CHRISTIAN HEROES: THEN & NOW

JOHN FLYNN

Into the Never Never

CHRISTIAN HEROES: THEN & NOW

JOHN FLYNN

Into the
Never Never

JANET & GEOFF BENGE

P.O. BOX 55787   SEATTLE, WA 98155

YWAM Publishing is the publishing ministry of Youth With A Mission (YWAM), an international missionary organization of Christians from many denominations dedicated to presenting Jesus Christ to this generation. To this end, YWAM has focused its efforts in three main areas: (1) training and equipping believers for their part in fulfilling the Great Commission (Matthew 28:19), (2) personal evangelism, and (3) mercy ministry (medical and relief work).

For a free catalog of books and materials, call (425) 771-1153 or (800) 922-2143. Visit us online at www.ywampublishing.com.

John Flynn: Into the Never Never

Published by YWAM Publishing
a ministry of Youth With A Mission
P.O. Box 55787, Seattle, WA 98155-0787

Library of Congress Cataloging-in-Publication Data

Names: Benge, Janet, 1958– author.
Title: John Flynn : into the never never / Janet and Geoff Benge.
Description: Seattle : YWAM Publishing, 2016. | Series: Christian heroes: then & now | Includes bibliographical references.
Identifiers: LCCN 2015047972 | ISBN 9781576588987 (pbk.)
Subjects: LCSH: Flynn, John, 1880–1951. | Missionaries—Australia—Biography. | Australian Inland Mission.
Classification: LCC BV3667.F5 B46 2016 | DDC 266/.793092--dc23
LC record available at http://lccn.loc.gov/2015047972

ISBN 978-1-57658-898-7 (paperback)
ISBN 978-1-57658-645-7 (e-book)

First printing 2016

Printed in the United States of America

This book is dedicated to
Hudson Salisbury (1927–2015)
of Upper Hutt, New Zealand.

As with John Flynn, the spiritual
well-being of others was always at
the forefront of Hudson's mind.

CHRISTIAN HEROES: THEN & NOW

Adoniram Judson	Jacob DeShazer
Amy Carmichael	Jim Elliot
Betty Greene	John Flynn
Brother Andrew	John Wesley
Cameron Townsend	John Williams
Clarence Jones	Jonathan Goforth
Corrie ten Boom	Klaus-Dieter John
Count Zinzendorf	Lillian Trasher
C. S. Lewis	Loren Cunningham
C. T. Studd	Lottie Moon
David Bussau	Mary Slessor
David Livingstone	Mildred Cable
D. L. Moody	Nate Saint
Elisabeth Elliot	Paul Brand
Eric Liddell	Rachel Saint
Florence Young	Rowland Bingham
Francis Asbury	Samuel Zwemer
George Müller	Sundar Singh
Gladys Aylward	Wilfred Grenfell
Hudson Taylor	William Booth
Ida Scudder	William Carey
Isobel Kuhn	

Available in paperback, e-book, and audiobook formats.
Unit study curriculum guides are available for select biographies.
www.HeroesThenAndNow.com

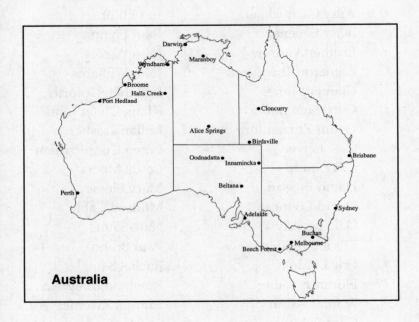

Australia

Contents

1. Braybrook. 11

2. Pupil Teacher. 19

3. Into the Mountains 27

4. Struck by a Lightning Bolt. 39

5. The Bushman's Companion 53

6. An Urgent Call, a Noble Vision 65

7. Challenges 77

8. Mantle of Safety 91

9. A Frustrating Lack of Vision 105

10. Hopelessly Bogged Down. 119

11. The Silence Is Broken 135

12. Advisors. 147

13. Around the World. 161

14. His "Mythical Self". 171

15. At His Finest 183

16. A Man Sent from God 197

    Bibliography 203

Chapter 1

Braybrook

Eleven-year-old John Flynn helped his older brother carry the dresser from their bedroom and out the door of their simple clapboard house. Once outside they lifted the dresser onto the wagon. It was moving day for the Flynn family. John and his father, Thomas, and John's fourteen-year-old brother, Eugene, and thirteen-year-old sister, Rosetta, were moving about seventy miles east of Snake Valley, Victoria, to the town of Braybrook, ten miles west of Melbourne.

As John heaved the solid pine furniture onto the wagon, he tried to sort out his feelings about moving again. He figured he'd done more moving than most boys his age, mainly because his mother, Rosetta, had died during childbirth when he was two years old. The baby had died two weeks later. John could not remember his mother, her funeral, or his baby brother. All he could remember was going to live with one set of relatives after another following his mother's death.

John knew what his mother looked like. His father had bought three silver lockets, placed a photograph of his wife inside each one, and given them to his children. Normally John kept his locket in a box beside his bed, but on special days, like today, he wore it around his neck. John wished he could remember his mother. Eugene and Rosetta had told him that she had been a kind woman and had beautiful auburn hair. And on the rarest occasions his father would talk about her, describing her beautiful singing voice and Irish lilt.

John packed up the last few things from the bedroom. "Do you have everything?" his father asked, entering the room.

John nodded as he stuffed his prize rabbit skins into a duffle bag. "Dad, will they have rabbits in Braybrook?"

Thomas Flynn chuckled. "There's nowhere in Australia safe from rabbits, son. You can have your fill of hunting them wherever you go."

John smiled. Rabbit hunting was one of his favorite pastimes. He loved to quietly stalk the pastureland outside town, creep up on unsuspecting rabbits, and shoot them with his .22-caliber rifle. And, as his father had pointed out, there was no shortage of rabbits in Australia. There had been no rabbits in the country before the arrival of Europeans, who brought rabbits with them from England. Now rabbits were everywhere throughout the countryside. They were considered a pest, since they ate the crops growing in farmers' fields and the vegetables in people's gardens.

Soon it was time to leave Snake Valley behind. John and his two siblings piled into the front of the wagon. Strangely, John was the only one of the three who had lived near a big city before. After his mother's death, his father had sent him to stay with his grandparents in the Sydney suburb of Summer Hill. One of John's earliest memories was sitting on the floor at the Methodist Sunday school in Summer Hill, singing with a large group of children. John had liked living with his grandparents, but in due course his father had brought him back home to live with him and the older children. Over the years, the three children and their father had forged a close-knit family. Now they were all headed to Braybrook, where Thomas was to be the principal at the first public school in the area.

John knew that the move was partly for the benefit of his older brother. Eugene was a brilliant student, and from Braybrook he would have the opportunity to attend University High School in Melbourne to prepare himself for college. For his part, John wasn't too worried about where he lived, as long as he could go rabbit hunting and ramble in the countryside. Although his father and brother loved nothing better than to sit and read long history and literature books, John much preferred to be outdoors with the sun beating on his back, his rifle tucked under his arm. Something about nature—the rolling country-side where cows and sheep grazed and kangaroos, wallabies, and emus roamed—made him feel free and alive.

The wagon swayed and lurched as the Flynns rode along, and soon everyone and everything was covered with a layer of red dust. John was glad when they reached Braybrook. However, many things about the new place surprised him. John had imag-ined living on the outskirts of a city, a place with paved roads and streetlamps. Instead he found him-self in a grimy town. Braybrook was the junction for the railroad lines that joined Melbourne—along with its ports in Williamstown and Newport—to Ballarat and Adelaide in the west and Bendigo in the north. As a result, it was a hub for industry, and many fac-tories dotted the landscape. Like their home in Snake Valley, the Flynns' new house had no running water and no sewage system. The wastewater gathered in puddles on the lower lying streets of the town, and once a week a worker shoveled lime powder onto the streets to reduce the smell.

Within a year of the Flynns' arrival in Braybrook, the area was struck with a typhoid fever epidemic that claimed the lives of a number of the town's resi-dents. Thankfully, no one in the Flynn household caught the disease. Soon after the typhoid epidemic, an economic depression hit the area. Money was short, and many people lost their jobs.

The depression had some effect on the Flynns.

Now the rabbits John hunted became a vital part of the family's dinner menu. John also sold the rabbit skins to a local tannery. His sister, Rosetta, soon became an expert at cooking rabbit, and any extra meat was given to needy neighbors. John also speared eels in Kororoit Creek and hunted for wild mushrooms for the dinner table.

When John roamed the plain that surrounded Braybrook, he seldom saw another human being. But one day as he combed the grasslands hunting rabbits, he spotted a man in his late twenties riding on horseback. The man wore a three-piece suit and a wide-brimmed felt hat. A gold watch chain dangled from his vest pocket. John frowned. Someone that well dressed was clearly out of place in the grasslands around Braybrook. As the man rode closer, John recognized the rider's outsized mustache from a photo he had seen. The man was Hugh Victor McKay. Everyone in town knew that this wealthy man was scouting the area for a site to build his Sunshine Harvester machines. Given the hard economic times, John knew that Braybrook was eager to have such a factory built in the area to provide jobs.

"Hello, lad," Mr. McKay said as he approached John. "Any luck with the hunting?"

"Not yet, sir," John replied politely. "I was just getting started. Over that rise is a rocky patch where I often have luck."

"Oh, you should keep that under your hat," Mr. McKay laughed. "You wouldn't want me beating you over there."

John smiled. He liked the man's easy manner.

"What's your name, lad?" Mr. McKay asked.

"John, John Flynn, sir. My father's the local school principal."

"Ah, Thomas Flynn. I've heard good reports of him. He also preaches at the local Presbyterian church, doesn't he?"

"Yes," John replied.

"That's what I like to see, good solid Christian families here in these parts. Please tell him Hugh McKay sends his greetings. We might be neighbors soon."

"Yes, sir," John said.

John watched Mr. McKay ride on across the rolling grassland. Hugh McKay was one of the richest men in Victoria, and he had just told John he might be moving next door. John could hardly believe he had met this important Australian.

In Braybrook, life had fallen into a steady pattern for the Flynn family. Eugene went off to attend University High School in the Melbourne suburb of Carlton, and John took over the job of chopping wood for the stove. By now Rosetta was doing most of the housework and cooking for the family.

When John turned sixteen, he began attending University High School, while Eugene went on to college to train as a teacher. John was not a natural student and had to work hard to make good grades. Because he knew how important this was to his father, he spent many hours poring over his textbooks. He passed his final exams at high school in 1898, which qualified him to go on to college. In his recommendation for John, the high school principal wrote, "John matriculated [passed his exams] within sixteen months. . . . This was due to his commendable industry and perseverance, as well as to his intellectual ability. He is one of the most trustworthy, painstaking and upright pupils this school has had for some time."

John could tell that his father was delighted with the recommendation. Both of Thomas's sons were doing well with their education. Eugene had just earned his teaching certificate and was destined for a bright career. Although no one knew where John would end up, his school reports showed he had the right work ethic to get wherever he wanted to go.

That summer, the Flynn family spent the Christmas holiday together. During this time John had to decide what he was going to do in the coming year. It was hard to imagine more study. He wanted to be free of all that, but he knew that his father would not approve. Education was very important to Thomas. John wished that he were more like Eugene, who was about to embark upon a teaching career at a city school. However, in early February 1899, Eugene began to feel ill with a stomachache and high fever. Could it be typhoid fever? John and his father took Eugene to the hospital in Melbourne, but within days Eugene was dead.

The Flynn family and the local community were shocked. Eugene Flynn had had such a bright future ahead of him, and now at age twenty-two his life was over. His funeral was held on February 16, and John sat numb through the service. He could scarcely take it in. Eugene had always been a kind and attentive big brother. Life seemed very fragile to John. "Work while it is day, for the night cometh when no man can work," the officiating minister said as Eugene's coffin was lowered into the ground. John wondered what kind of work he should do. What work would be worthwhile? John wasn't sure, but he knew he needed to spend his life doing something that would make a difference in the lives of others.

Chapter 2

Pupil Teacher

John decided to follow in his brother's footsteps and become a teacher. He took a position as a pupil teacher with the Victorian Education Department. This meant that John was a teacher in training who would receive on-the-job instruction by going from school to school and observing teachers in action and teaching his own lessons under supervision. He would then take an examination to become a certified teacher. John was well suited for the combination of work and study, and he had no trouble passing the examination.

During his training, John had been based in schools around the Melbourne area, which allowed him to continue living at home in Braybrook. But in the winter of 1901, John was assigned to the school in Hazelwood South, about one hundred miles southeast of Braybrook. Living in the country again was quite a change for John. He stayed with a farming family at Eel Hole Corner and decided to spend his spare time exploring the countryside. The way to do this, John decided, was by bicycle, and he bought himself the best bike he could afford with the money he earned. It was a sturdy sports bike with a sprung leather saddle, mudguards on each wheel, and a carbide lamp for riding at night. John also bought himself a new .22-caliber rifle, which he maintained meticulously. With his new rifle slung over his shoulder, he was soon riding fifty, sometimes seventy-five, miles on Saturdays through the rolling countryside around Hazelwood. He rode over tracks that led through groves of trees and out alongside fields where cows grazed on the lush grass.

John started a Sunday school that many local children began attending. He was startled to learn that many of the children had not been baptized and most had never even seen a Bible. He also discovered that teaching simple hymns to the children, who had no church background, was a challenge.

Often, as he rode through the countryside, John thought about the meaning of life. He had always felt that he was a Christian, and he always tried to please God, but what did that really mean for his life? Lately he'd been aware of an unmistakable impression that God wanted him to become a Presbyterian pastor, even though it involved more study. Pursuing this idea presented John with a pressing problem. John had been unable to save any money on his small pupil-teacher allowance, and he knew that his father could not help him finance all the education needed to become a pastor. John began praying that if God wanted him to be a pastor, God would show him the way ahead.

At the end of his six-month teaching assignment in Hazelwood South, John headed back to Braybrook for Christmas. In February 1902, following the summer school vacation, John was assigned to teach at West Hawthorne State School, which meant he could live at home with his father and Rosetta. At twenty-one years of age, John was fit and strong. He combined his Christian faith with his love of the outdoors, becoming leader of the Footscray Young Men's Bible Class, where, along with teaching Bible studies, he organized hikes, bike rides, and fishing expeditions for the group.

Once he received his teaching certificate, John began looking around for other ways to serve people. He found an advertisement in the newspaper for a first aid course being run by the St. John's Association in Melbourne. John paid his ten shillings and took the course. He loved every minute of it. He learned how to use a tourniquet to stop bleeding, how to splint broken legs and arms, how to care for someone who had been knocked unconscious, what to do about snakebites, how to help someone who was choking, and how to treat common illnesses. Along with studying the guidebook that came with the course, John took careful notes with which he could refresh his memory when he might have to deal with a particular medical emergency. John passed the first aid course with "much credit."

Another hobby soon captured John's interest—photography. John bought a camera and began taking photographs, fiddling with the exposure and aperture settings to see the effect each had on the final image. Of course, before he could view his photos, John had to develop the film. He bought the various chemicals and equipment needed for the developing process and taught himself how to develop film and print photographs in a dark cupboard in the house. Before long he also taught himself how to make enlargements. John and his camera became inseparable.

With his new hobby and the Footscray Young Men's Bible Class to run, John had more than enough to keep him busy on weekends. And he was kept busy during the week with a class of forty students to teach at West Hawthorne State School.

In September 1902, as the first calves were being born out on the farms, John came up with a plan for his summer vacation in December that would combine the things he loved the most. He decided to take a long bike trip, photographing what he saw along the way. To cover the cost of the trip, he decided to write articles about his adventure and sell them and his photographs to the local newspaper, the *Footscray Advertiser.*

After arranging things with the newspaper, John set himself the challenge of designing a tent. Since he would carry everything with him on his bicycle during the trip, he needed a tent that was small, lightweight, and easy for one person to put up. Using lightweight canvas, John fashioned a tent seven feet by five feet with a grommet in the center into which fitted a single pole consisting of two broom handles held together with a metal ring. The pole held the center of the tent aloft, and the sides were fastened to the ground with pegs. Not only was the tent light, but also, with a blanket and other provisions, it could be rolled up into a swag and carried on John's back as he rode his bicycle.

Once school ended for the summer in early December 1902, John was off on his five-hundred-mile adventure. He loaded two small cooking pots, a tomahawk to chop firewood, food supplies, his camera and film, pen and paper, and other necessities into a bag that hung from the handlebars of his bike. Attached to the back of his saddle was a water bag. Altogether, John carried thirty pounds of gear with him on the bicycle. One of the last things he stowed away in the front bag was his St. John's first aid handbook and a triangle bandage. Then John swung his swag and his rifle over his shoulder and peddled off.

John headed in a southwesterly direction to Geelong and then west to Inverleigh before heading northwest. At night he would unroll his swag, erect the tent, and set to work cooking dinner, which often consisted of rabbit stew and damper, a bread made from flour and water and cooked on the campfire coals. In the morning John would take down the tent, roll up his swag, repack the bag onto his handlebars, and head off along the track.

Occasionally John would pass a person riding on horseback or in a wagon. He would stop and talk awhile, hoping to extract from the person some interesting local tidbits to enliven the articles he planned to write about his trip. He would also stop and take photographs to illustrate the articles.

At first the countryside was green and rolling and studded with healthy livestock, but as he rode deeper into the heart of Victoria, the land became parched and the livestock thin. This part of Victoria was in the grip of a drought, and John took a lot of photos and notes as he passed through it.

As he rode over the rough tracks, John thought about his future. He enjoyed being a teacher, but he still felt that God had called him to be a Presbyterian pastor. Yet he had to face the fact that he was no nearer to that goal. Even if he hadn't spent money on a bike and camera, what he could save from his meager salary would not get him very far in college. Something had to change so that he could undertake the study necessary to become a pastor.

When he reached Warracknabeal, John headed east, back toward Melbourne. He passed through Donald and St. Arnaud, located close to his birthplace, the small hamlet of Moliagul. Then he rode on to Bendigo, near the geographic center of Victoria. Bendigo had become the center of a major gold rush when gold was found in the area in 1851. By the time John peddled into town on his bicycle, the gold rush was well over and people were moving on. After photographing the sights of Bendigo, John set out on

the ninety-mile final leg of his ride southeast to Braybrook. As he approached the town of Woodend on a
Saturday evening, he spotted a horse tethered near a
tent at the side of the road. John slowed his bike and
rode around the horse. Moments later he was lying
flat on his back. As he scrambled to his feet, he discovered that wire netting had been stretched across
the road. He walked back to the tent, where an old
drover told him he'd laid out the wire netting to stop
his sheep from wandering.

John arrived home in Braybrook with many stories to tell from his adventure in the Victorian countryside. The first article about his trip appeared in the
January 10, 1903, edition of the *Footscray Advertiser*.
The money he was paid for the article and photographs barely covered the price of his film and developing chemicals. Many people complimented John
on his lively writing style, and he appreciated their
compliments. He enjoyed writing the articles. He just
wished doing so was more profitable.

As John was preparing for another year of teaching, one of the young men attending the Footscray
Young Men's Bible Class mentioned to him that he'd
seen an advertisement seeking young men to become
home missionaries. Intrigued, John looked into the
idea and discovered that the Presbyterian Church of
Victoria was desperately short of ministers for all the
new settlements opening across eastern Australia.
The denomination had come up with a plan similar to the pupil-teacher program. The Presbyterian
Church would pay any young man with a pastoral

calling to go to a pioneering area to preach the gospel and prepare the groundwork for the establishment of a local church. In return, the denomination offered correspondence courses to these home missionaries, who, if they passed the courses, had the chance to win a scholarship to Ormond College at the University of Melbourne.

Because it sounded like the kind of break John needed, he applied to the program immediately. In June 1903 he received an acceptance letter and a mission field. He was to be sent to a place named Beech Forest, in the Otway Mountains of southern Victoria. John hurried to the map to see exactly where his new home would be.

Chapter 3

Into the Mountains

H ey, mate, you looking for a job?"
John turned to see who was talking to him. It was a middle-aged man with deeply wrinkled, sunburned skin and bright blue eyes. "No," he replied. "Just somewhere to stay awhile."

The man looked at John quizzically. "You got your own job then, eh?"

John nodded. "In a way. I'm here with the Presbyterian Church."

"What church? There ain't no church around here for miles." The man shook his head. "Not that anyone round here would care. The pub's enough for most of us. It's hard work out here, boy. No place for city sissies and the like. Hard yakka, hard drinking, try to stay alive. That's how it is around here."

John smiled. "I'll keep that in mind," he said, patting his new horse, which he had bought in Colac, twenty-four miles north on the edge of the Otway Mountains. John had then plunged into the dense forest, following a muddy trail while avoiding the deep ruts made by wagons hauling huge tree trunks to the railhead at Colac. Now he stood on the only street in Beech Forest, a cluster of wooden houses in the heart of the Otway Mountains surrounded by a ring of clear-cut land. When he had first heard of his posting to the place, it had been nothing more than an isolated dot on the map. Now he was standing in the middle of the ramshackle town, his new mission field.

By nightfall John had found temporary lodging in a small house. As he lay on his horsehair mattress that night, he thought about his plan of action. His home mission field stretched to Laver Hill in the west and encompassed most of the Otway Mountains, an area studded with sawmills and small timber camps. The area included a few scattered farms, where settlers were trying to eke out an existence among the stumps of trees that had already been felled. It was immediately obvious to John that the men of this area—there were few women or children—were long on endurance and short on patience for Bible thumpers. John realized it would be useless to quote Bible verses to them or talk theology. He would need a different approach if he were to have any chance of communicating the gospel to the men. As he drifted off to sleep, he decided that the best thing would be to visit every part of his new mission field to learn about the locals' way of life and find out exactly what the people needed most.

The next morning John repacked his saddlebags with his camera at the top and set off. At the first saw-mill he came to, he introduced himself and asked if he could help out. The foreman laughed and pointed to a pit. John soon found himself on the end of a long saw at the bottom of the pit while another worker guided the other end of the saw from above. Together the men moved the saw back and forth, cutting enor-mous tree trunks into planks. Sawdust rained down on John as he worked, and soon it seemed to him that every muscle in his lanky body hurt. He wondered how the sawmill workers managed to do this for twelve to fourteen hours a day, day in and day out. Nonetheless, he stuck at it, and his efforts at pit saw-ing earned him the respect of the mill workers.

As he rode through the Otway Mountains, John would often stop to take photographs. Every twist of the trail brought a new vista, each, it seemed, more breathtaking than the last. Tall ash trees rose hundreds of feet straight up. Mingled among them were blue gums, blackwoods, myrtle, and beech. The trees formed a dense forest, amid which waterfalls cascaded down mossy rock faces. Ferns and orchids covered the ground. Bird life abounded with crim-son rosellas, eastern yellow robins, white-throated treecreepers, and white-browed scrubwrens. The birds' agitated chattering was usually a warning that a snake was nearby. Wombats, wallabies, kangaroos, and koalas lived among the trees.

Dotted amid this extraordinary beauty were the logging camps. Each time John entered one, he offered to work alongside the men. In exchange, the foreman usually offered him a camp bed for the night and a place at the dining hall table.

John soon adjusted to the hard physical labor, and he quickly learned how to get along with the timbermen, who loved to spin yarns. John could soon spin a good yarn with the best of them. At the dinner table he especially liked to tell stories from his five-hundred-mile bike trip around central Victoria.

All the while, John waited patiently for the right time to start a church service. It came soon enough. John was riding into a new timber camp when he saw a group of men huddled over something. Wondering what they were looking at, he dismounted and walked over. In the center of the group, a man lay groaning on a blanket.

"What happened?" John asked.

"A log rolled on him. We don't know what to do or how bad he's hurt," the nearest man replied.

"Maybe I can help," John said. "I know some first aid. Here, let me through. Give your mate some air."

The men stepped back obediently to let John through. The injured logger lay doubled up in pain. He was grasping his left arm and made no sound. *They're made tough out here,* John thought as he knelt beside the man.

"Let's just take a look at this," John said, reaching for the logger's arm. The man grimaced as John gently felt along the injured arm.

"Broken, that's for sure," John said. As he felt the man's abdomen and chest, John watched carefully for more signs of extreme pain but didn't see any. "I don't think he has internal injuries, thank the Lord," he said. "Someone get me some bandages from the right pocket of my saddlebag. I'll splint him up to immobilize the arm, and then you'll have to get him to the nearest doctor."

The men stood around as John used a snapped-off branch and the bandages to splint the man's broken arm.

"Pretty good job you did there, mate," one man said. "You rigged that thing up good and proper. How'd ya learn to do that?"

"First aid class, back in Braybrook," John said, standing up.

Another man extended his hand to shake John's. "I'm Mac, the foreman out here. Good thing you came along. None of us knows what to do at times like this, and sometimes it gets pretty dicey."

John suddenly had an idea. "How would you like me to give your men some basic first aid lessons? Then you could help each other."

"Sounds good," Mac said. "I'll even come myself. Now and again you can teach an old dog a new trick or two. We could clear off the dining hall table after dinner. Would that work okay?"

"Great," John said. "I could cover the basics in about four one-hour sessions."

"You're on," Mac said, smiling. "See you at dinner."

That night after dinner, John stood in front of twenty-five men. He supposed that few if any of them had gone past primary school, but after the accident that day, they were ready to learn. Oil lamps flooded the room with a flickering light as John started his lecture. Since their mate had broken his arm, John began with how to tell if a limb was broken and then explained how to splint broken arms and legs. He moved on to the many uses of the triangle bandage and then discussed the various ways to stop bleeding. He kept the session lively by telling stories about accidents and injuries, some of them quite gruesome, he'd encountered or heard about. He told stories of men bitten by snakes or attacked by wild animals and stories of people whose wounds had become gangrenous because they had not been treated properly. The men loved it. John also used some of the men to illustrate his talks, and he discovered that some of them were real actors. They laughed and kidded with each other as they acted out the various types of injuries John described.

On Saturday night as he neared the end of his last lecture of the first aid course, John said, "Men, you've been a great group. I think you have learned a lot and made living out here a lot safer for all of you. It's been a pleasure to show you some ways to patch up a body, but we are more than just bodies. I am in the business of teaching first aid for the soul as well, and tomorrow morning I'll be telling you about that right here. You are all invited to come and listen."

Many of the men nodded, and John smiled to himself. He'd found a way to get through to the men: help them with their physical needs first and then challenge them on their spiritual ones.

The following morning most of the men showed up for a simple church service in the dining room. They sang "Amazing Grace," which John thought would be the most well known hymn. He wished they had hymnals to pass around, but that wasn't likely at a timber camp. Following the singing of the hymn, he did the same thing he'd done at his first aid lectures. He told simple stories to illustrate the points he was making about Jesus Christ and the gospel. The stories held the men's interest and made them feel like John was one of them. After this experience, John knew he'd discovered the way to get through to the men out in the forest. He began offering first aid classes wherever he went. Soon he was a welcome sight along the trails of the Otway Mountains and was invited to hold church services in tents, huts, and timber camps.

It was on one of his itinerating adventures that John got to use first aid on himself. He was visiting one of the remote farms scattered along the trail when his horse tripped on a tree root. The horse reared up and threw John off its back. As he fell to the ground, John hit his mouth on a branch. Blood gushed everywhere. The horse calmed down and stood silently awaiting instructions. John lay still for a moment trying to assess what was wrong. Blood was coming from his upper lip. Feeling along the outline of his lip, he realized that the branch had ripped his lip open all the way up to his nose. No wonder his lip was bleeding so much! Slowly he stood up and pulled a rolled bandage from his saddlebag, pressing it tight against his lip to stanch the bleeding. Eventually he remounted his horse and set out for Colac, where he found a doctor who could sew up his split upper lip.

The incident left John with a permanent scar, making him look like he was born with a cleft lip that had been repaired. John took it in stride. Most men he met along the way out in the bush had some scar or other and a yarn to explain it. Now he did too.

John settled into a hut of his own in Beech Forest. It was a very simple affair, but it had a table and an oil lamp, the two things he needed most to study his correspondence lessons. When he was not riding a circuit of the various timber camps and hamlets of the Otway Mountains, John studied far into the night. He also took time to develop his photographs, a number of which he turned into lantern slides. Some of these he hand colored following instructions he found in a magazine.

John's attention to his correspondence lessons paid off, and he passed his first-year home mission examinations. After John had spent eighteen months based at Beech Forest, the Presbyterian Home Missions Committee decided to reassign him to Buchan in East Gippsland in southeastern Victoria.

John was sorry to leave Beech Forest and the friends he had made there. But if he wanted to become a pastor, it was time for him to move on for more training on a different home mission field. On the way to his new posting, John traveled through Braybrook, where he stayed with his father and sister.

Buchan, located in the mountains 220 miles east of Melbourne, was very similar to Beech Forest. Much of the area had been logged, and now settlers were trying to eke out a living on farms throughout the area, grazing their sheep and cattle among the tree stumps. Much of the land was hilly, and the farmers often found themselves having to deal with bushfires and famine. Those living in the valleys, through which numerous rivers flowed from the mountains, experienced floods. The main river was the Snowy River. The scenery of East Gippsland was every bit as magnificent as that of the Otway Mountains. John soon had his camera focused on the landscape.

John used the same approach he'd used in the Otway Mountains to win the favor of the local people. He helped out wherever he could and gave first aid lessons. He also gave public slide viewings on his magic lantern to help enliven the monotony of life in the mountains of East Gippsland. At first he showed his slide presentation entitled "How the Land Was Won," which told the story of the timbermen and pioneer farmers in the Beech Forest area. The magic lantern shows were an instant success, drawing eager crowds. Even more people showed up when John put together a slide show on East Gippsland called "The Snowy River."

After a year in the area, John rented a small house in Buchan so that his sister, Rosetta, could come stay with him. Rosetta was eager to see what he did and wanted to help with the Sunday school John had started. She had a flair for writing, and she sent home interesting letters to their local church.

Through his unassuming ways and willingness to help out wherever he could, John made many friends throughout the area. One of them was a man named Frank Moon, an amateur explorer from the small town of Gelantipy. One day Frank came bounding into John's house. "Flynn, I've made a most incredible find. You must come and photograph it."

"What is it?" John asked.

"I blasted the granite wall of a canyon with gelignite, and it opened up an amazing cave. I went down into it using a rope and a candle to light my way. What I saw was unbelievable: stalactites and stalagmites and great pillars of rock in a huge cavern that seemed to branch off in the distance in all directions. You must come now," Frank urged.

John gathered up his camera, film, and some strong flashlights so that he could take photos underground in the dark and followed Frank. He was not disappointed. The cavern was truly huge and amazing, just as Frank had said. And when he developed the photographs he had taken in the cavern, John was stunned. The images were dramatic and revealed an underground landscape unlike anything John had ever before experienced. As he looked at the photos, John was reminded of something Frank had said to him at the cavern: "This cave could make a huge difference in such a poor area as this."

"How so?" John had asked him.

"Tourists. This cavern could attract thousands of visitors a year to Buchan."

John's mind began to whirl with the possibilities. If it was handled right, the Buchan cave could create many opportunities for the locals. John began to wonder what he could do to help make that happen. Two things immediately came to mind. The first was to publish his photographs of the cavern, and the other was to support the East Gippsland Railway League that was lobbying for a railroad to be built through the area, a railroad that could bring tourists from all over the country.

The two ideas converged to take John to Melbourne in October 1906 with a delegation from the East Gippsland Railway League. In Melbourne, John got to meet the premier of Victoria, Sir Thomas Bent, and show him his photographs of the Buchan cave. Sir Thomas was impressed as he examined the photographs one by one and promised to protect the cave and take a serious look at the need for a railroad through the area. John had expected to feel nervous giving his presentation to the highest official in the state, but surprisingly he didn't feel that way at all. In fact, he was invigorated by it.

While in Melbourne, John made the rounds of the local newspapers, the *Weekly Times*, the *Leader*, and the *Australasian*. All three papers bought his photographs of the cave, which allowed him to buy more photographic supplies. While John realized he would never get rich off his hobby, he was glad that his photographs had played a valuable part in helping outsiders understand the beauty of the cave and the need to preserve it.

By the end of 1906, John had been in East Gippsland for almost two years. In that time, he'd ridden on horseback through the entire Snowy River gorge and explored more of the land than anyone he knew. He had also continued to conscientiously apply himself to his studies and passed the Presbyterian Home Missions Committee's final examinations. In so doing, he had won a place at Ormond College for the following year. But now that it was time to leave for Melbourne, John wondered how difficult it would be to leave his wandering, preaching life behind and spend the next three years studying in the city.

Chapter 4

Struck by a Lightning Bolt

The voice of his lecturer faded away as John sat staring out the window into the courtyard of the ornate stone building. John's mind swirled, pondering whether he was too old for studying. He looked around the room. At twenty-six years of age, he was surely one of the oldest students in college. Was it too late to grasp Hebrew syntax or Greek conjugations? There were so many more interesting things to think about, such as the boys at Montague. In addition to keeping up with his theological studies at Ormond College, John had been assigned as the home missionary for that inner-city suburb.

The conditions many of the children lived under in Montague were as harsh as any John had seen out in the countryside. John was particularly concerned about the teenage boys. Many of them skipped school and had no jobs. They wandered around the slums, stealing things and bullying the younger children. What they needed was something constructive to do, something exciting. But what? Suddenly John had an idea: *find a way to get a boat.* He wrote a note at the top of his lecture notes. That was it. If the boys had a boat, they could row it up and down the Yarra River and its tributaries. Such activity would teach them to work together as a team and expose them to what lay beyond their own doorsteps as they navigated the river.

As soon as class was over, John began asking his friends where he might get a boat. One friend suggested he try a local shipping company run by a Scotsman. Then the friend laughed and said, "But you don't have a chance of talking a boat out of old Jock McGregor. He might be a good Presbyterian, but he's a mean one. He's never let a penny slip through his fingers."

That night John prayed that God would give him the right words to say to Mr. McGregor. The next day after class, he headed down to the docks. He found Mr. McGregor in his office, surrounded by papers and bills of lading. The man looked surprised to see John, and more so when he learned that John had come to ask for a free boat for the teenage boys of Montague. Undeterred, John continued in his easy manner, telling the Scotsman all the ways boating would help the boys get focus in their lives.

"I agree with ye," Mr. McGregor said when John had finished his pitch. "The devil makes work for idol hands. Let's get these boys a boat. Where would you like it delivered?"

John chuckled with delight. He had no previous experience with boats. Now he needed to learn to row convincingly—and fast—so he could teach the boys how to do it.

The boat was a great success and, John had to confess, far more interesting than his studies. He continued to struggle with most of his subjects. He was passing systematic theology and apologetics, scraping by in church history, and failing in Hebrew and Greek.

One day John was called to the office of the director of Home Missions for Victoria. He was expecting a stern reprimand over his studies, but the Reverend Donald Cameron had something else in mind. "I see languages are difficult for you," he said.

"Yes," John agreed. "I keep trying, but I get farther behind."

"Oh well," Mr. Cameron said. "I've heard about your magic lantern shows. Tell me about them."

John was glad to get off the topic of his grades and onto something he really cared about. He told the director about "How the Land Was Won" and "The Snowy River," how he had put them together using photos he'd taken, how people had flocked to see the magic lantern shows, and how effective the shows had been in interesting people in spiritual matters and getting them to come to church meetings.

Mr. Cameron leaned in and said to John, "You have to finish the year out, but the good news is that all your grades are combined. So if you keep doing well in the things you can do, perhaps you can use those grades to get yourself to a passing grade in Greek and Hebrew." Then standing, he reached over and patted John on the back. "Don't worry. God doesn't make us all the same. There's a special place for you somewhere. It's your job to discover where. Don't give up. I'm keeping an eye on you, John."

Not long afterward Mr. Cameron invited John to tour the Warracknabeal district with him, one of the districts John had peddled through on his bike tour of central Victoria five years before. John's assignment was to give his magic lantern presentations and encourage the churches in the area to become involved in sending more home missionaries to remote areas of Victoria. The assignment suited John perfectly. He was back among rural working people, spinning yarns and offering advice and spiritual counsel when it seemed appropriate.

In March 1908 John plunged back into his studies at Ormond College. He knew his biblical language skills would never be great, but he hoped his combined grades would be good enough to let him skate in under the wire, as they had the year before.

John was as busy in his second year as he had been in his first. The Montague boys went rowing every Saturday afternoon, and he could see a real change in their attitudes. Some of them had even started going to the local church youth group.

When he was not working with the boys or studying, John tried to imagine what lay ahead for him. Given his difficulties studying, he couldn't really see himself preparing sermons and preaching month after month in a church. In fact, he decided to slow down his studies, choosing to spread his second year of study over two years.

As 1909 began, John still had two years of study left at college to earn his divinity degree. But pressure began to mount for him to make a decision about what he would do when he graduated. Since he couldn't really see himself as a pastor in a local parish, John began to wonder if he might be better suited to be a missionary in a foreign country. The Presbyterian Church in Victoria had a mission in Korea that was desperately short of personnel. An appeal was made to students at Ormond College for those willing to go to Korea as missionaries at the end of their theological studies. The students were asked to raise their hands, but no one put a hand up. John looked around the room and then gingerly raised his. "I'll go," he said, "but only if you are still short of volunteers when I finish my training."

In mid-1909, however, soon after John had volunteered to go to Korea as a missionary, his eyes were opened to new possibilities. John received a letter from the editor of the *Messenger*, the Presbyterian Church magazine in Victoria. The letter was from a Mrs. Jessie Litchfield of West Arm in Australia's Northern Territory. John began to read:

I received some copies of your monthly paper, and I am writing now some news of this lonely land.

I am eighty miles from a town by land, twenty by sea, three miles from the nearest white woman, two miles from the nearest white man. Chinese and blacks [Aborigines] are my nearest neighbors. There are three churches in Darwin, Church of England, Roman Catholic and Methodist. There is also a convent conducted by Roman Catholic sisters. . . .

The Methodist preacher paid four visits to West Arm last year. This year no one will come. There are no other ministers in the Northern Territory—500,000 square miles of country with 1,500 whites, 2,000 Chinese and 5,000 blacks living here.

John stopped reading for a moment, taken aback by the numbers he'd just read. How big was 500,000 square miles? He did some quick math. All of Australia consisted of about three million square miles, so Mrs. Litchfield was talking about one-sixth of the country, in which only eighty-five hundred people lived! It seemed incredible. John checked his math; it was correct. There were so few people spread over the Northern Territory that it made sparsely populated rural Victoria seem like it was having a population explosion.

Mrs. Litchfield went on in her letter to write about the social problems of having so few European women in the Northern Territory. Many children of mixed race were running around whom no one seemed to want to claim. On top of this, alcohol and other drugs were readily available and were the cause of many accidents and deaths. Mrs. Litchfield concluded her letter with, "Why cannot the Presbyterian Church send up a missionary to the Northern Territory? . . . He would do good, if he were a man who put Christ first, and who worked for the good of others, and spared neither time nor money nor labour in the cause of Christ."

By the time John had finished reading the letter it was as though he'd been struck by a lightning bolt. *Of course,* he thought. *God is calling me to the inland of Australia, not to Korea. I'm the man Jessie Litchfield is asking for.*

During the next week, John felt such a sense of peace and certainty about this calling that he wrote to his father telling him of his change of heart. Then he wrote to Mrs. Litchfield asking her many questions about living in the Australian outback. While he awaited answers to his letters, John set to work studying a large map of Australia. He was amazed by what he discovered. Not just the Northern Territory, but two-thirds of Australia—two million square miles—was sparsely populated. Most of the country's population lived in settlements or on farms located within an approximately two-hundred-mile-wide strip of land along the east and southeast coast. The arid interior of the country that extended all the way to the Indian Ocean in the west and the Arafura

Sea in the north was virtually empty. Stretched across this near-empty landscape were the small rural farms and hamlets that Jessie Litchfield had described in her letter. John wondered why he hadn't studied a map of Australia more closely in the past. He'd had no idea just how vast the outback of the country was.

John bought a copy of a best-selling book released the year before. The book, entitled *We of the Never Never*, was an autobiographical novel of author Jeannie Gunn's life and experiences at Elsey Station near Mataranka in the Northern Territory. In 1902 Jeannie became the first white woman to settle in the Mataranka area, where her husband was a partner in the Elsey cattle station on the Roper River, three hundred miles south of Darwin. At first Jeannie was discouraged from accompanying her husband to the station. She was a woman and as such would be out of place at Elsey. Unperturbed, she set out, and the book described her journey and settling in the Never Never, as the vast Australian outback was often referred to. Reading *We of the Never Never* confirmed for John everything Jessie Litchfield had written about in her letter.

John also began spending a lot of time with Donald Cameron, discussing ways in which the Presbyterian Church could help the inlanders living in remote areas.

In the meantime, the summer holidays loomed. With his combined grades, John scraped through yet another year of college and planned a mission trip for the summer. This time he intended to minister to shearers in western Victoria and southeastern South Australia. Shearers were an itinerant group who traveled from sheep farm to sheep farm, where they would stay long enough to shear a farmer's sheep before moving on. Because they were so mobile, the shearers rarely put down roots in a community and had virtually no interaction or affiliation with a church. A shearer's life was usually one of hard physical labor and hard drinking.

John set out from Melbourne by train, but in the course of the trip, he also traveled by stagecoach and on horseback. On one occasion he even got to ride in one of the motorcars that were beginning to pop up on Australian roads. When people asked him what that was like, John told them that the car ride was so windy it nearly blew his ears off, but it was better than riding in a stagecoach behind two tired horses. Along the way he held meetings in churches, at farm homesteads, and in shearing sheds. In churches he preached direct Christian messages. His presentations at the homesteads and in the shearing sheds usually included first aid lessons, sometimes one of his magic lantern shows, and a discussion about spiritual matters.

Upon reaching Hamilton, Victoria, John met the Reverend Andrew Barber, the local Presbyterian pastor. The two men became fast friends, and John stayed in the manse with Andrew. While John was there, a local man delivered a box of Christian tracts for him to use in his mission to the shearers. John read one of the tracts and then declared, "This is not good. I can't use these. They're written for people in the city, and especially those who know church terminology. The average shearer is not going to understand these tracts."

Andrew looked over one of the tracts and agreed with John. The two of them talked late into the night about the kind of material that would relate to and be helpful for shearers and others living in rural settings. John explained that the shearers and others who heard his first aid lectures had asked him to write them down and make them available. He also recounted how a shearer told him that he and several other men had to bury one of their friends while working out in the bush. They would have liked to have given their friend a Christian burial but had no idea how to do so. Instead they had sung "Auld Lang Syne" and "For He's a Jolly Good Fellow" as they covered the grave with dirt. "Imagine a pamphlet that had first aid instruction in it as well as a description of a simple Christian burial service and prayers for different occasions and also talked openly about Jesus Christ and the gospel," John said.

The idea intrigued Andrew, who encouraged John to write something like that, which could be given to people living in the bush.

In March 1910, after three months of traveling and giving talks to shearers, John entered his fourth and what he hoped would be his final year of college. His time among the shearers had stimulated many ideas, and once again he had trouble concentrating in class. During lectures his mind kept wandering to what he could do to help break the sense of isolation in the outback. He hit upon the idea of mailing books and magazines to people out there. The people could read them and then pass them on whenever they saw another human being. Better yet, John could ask other people to send their used reading materials to the outback. And so the Mailbag League was formed.

John asked his sister, Rosetta, and their child-hood friend Esther Mahood to help him organize the league. Rosetta was particularly useful, since she wrote a regular column for the *Messenger* under the pen name of Cousin Charlotte, in which she often tackled social issues. Soon books were pouring in to John, who spent many hours wrapping and address-ing them to any outback address he could get ahold of. Every parcel was mailed with a prayer and a hope that one day he would get to meet the people who would be receiving the books.

Esther arranged for John to talk to the Presbyte-rian Women's Mission Union of Victoria about the Mailbag League. The women caught the vision for sending books and literature to remote areas. In fact, they willingly took over the responsibility of manag-ing the league for John so that he could get back to concentrating on his studies.

Not long after this, the Reverend Ernest Bald-win came to lecture at Ormond College. He was the Smith of Dunesk missioner, the only permanent Presbyterian missionary within Australia. While the mission name was strange, John soon learned that it was named after Mrs. Henrietta Smith of Dunesk,

Scotland. In 1894 Mrs. Smith had donated the money for the Presbyterian Church of South Australia to establish a mission to benefit those living in the Australian outback. The mission was established at Beltana, about 350 miles north of Adelaide in South Australia.

John sat fascinated as he listened to Mr. Baldwin describe his mission work at Beltana. It was an adventurous and rugged life that saw him spending most of his time away from Beltana traveling throughout the Never Never, far from any town or road, offering friendship and spiritual help to anyone he met.

"I've heard you're interested in going into the Never Never," Mr. Baldwin said to John at the end of his lecture. "Mr. Cameron tells me you make quite a splash with your magic lantern shows and your knack for getting along with anyone. I'm getting married next year and leaving Beltana. We'll be needing a replacement for me, someone who knows how to make his way with all sorts of people and can preach the gospel in a way that bushmen can hear it. You just might be that person."

John laughed. "I have to graduate first. That will be difficult enough."

"You'll be hearing from me. Keep up your studies. You're nearly through," Mr. Baldwin said, shaking John's hand.

Following Ernest Baldwin's lecture, John headed to the library to learn all he could about the Smith of Dunesk missioner's job. He discovered that although the mission was based in Beltana, there were no boundaries as to how far its work extended into the outback. John realized that if he took the missioner's job, there was no reason that he could not cover as much of the outback as he wanted.

John also discovered a few discouraging things about the work of the mission. Since its founding, there had been six Smith of Dunesk missioners, and apparently most of them had left with little success. In fact, a past missioner, Frank Rolland, wrote, "The odds against religion in this district are so heavy that unless God works miracles as great as making deaf men hear and dead men live, the mission to the Far North is hopeless and ridiculous." *Not promising words*, John thought.

Nonetheless, John wrote to his father, seeking his opinion about whether he should take up the position with the Smith of Dunesk Mission. The reply John received was also discouraging. "As to going up to the Center of Australia and hiding yourself there for two years, I hope that won't come off. What is your sister to do? And what would become of you if you took ill? In that new country, a young fellow unused to the climate and life would be almost certain to take the typhoid fever as hundreds did in the west. Let someone else take the mission—a man of more years than yourself," Thomas Flynn wrote.

His father's letter was difficult for John to read, and John wondered what he should do now.

Chapter 5

The Bushman's Companion

After reading the letter from his father, John decided to pray about the situation. He then got on with the job at hand, his new brainchild: *The Bushman's Companion*. Since his conversation with Andrew Barber in Hamilton during his summer mission to the shearers, John had been taking notes on the kinds of things that would be interesting and useful to someone living out in the bush. He had also written to doctors, solicitors, other ministers, and people living in isolated rural areas, asking them for ideas that might be helpful that he could put in the new publication. John also persuaded the Home Mission Committee to set aside money to have the new book published. And so the Bush Publishing Fund was set up.

John continued to scrape by with his grades, even though he put most of his energy into writing *The Bushman's Companion*. "Cousin Charlotte" wrote a stirring article in the *Messenger* to help raise money to cover the cost of publishing and distributing *The Bushman's Companion*. As a result, the Bush Publishing Fund grew.

True to his word, Ernest Baldwin kept writing to John from Beltana. With each new letter, John became more convinced that he was called to minister in inland Australia. He came to see that in serving as the missionary in Beltana he would not be wasting two years of his life, as his father had thought. In fact, John was planning on making his time with the Smith of Dunesk Mission even more worthwhile. He accepted the missioner's position with the hope of using it as a springboard to creating a mission that would one day cover the entire Australian outback.

By the beginning of September 1910, John had completed writing and editing *The Bushman's Companion*, which was sent off to be printed. Two weeks later he was holding a copy of the new publication. The compact book with a blue linen cover was designed to fit easily into a pocket or saddlebag. John thumbed through the pages, and everything was in order. He breathed a sigh of relief. The job of writing and preparing the book was over.

The book contained an introduction by John, followed by a long section on first aid. It also had sections covering topics such as how to make a will and how to conduct a burial service. In addition, it included an introduction to the Mailbag League, a selection of Bible verses, prayers for various occasions, and the words to a number of hymns. The back of the book contained information on postal rates, pages on which to keep a cash account, and pages on which to jot down notes. The book also had a section John titled "A Ramble among Ideas." This section included quotes from John's favorite writers and poets that elaborated a set of ideals John thought men and women should strive to live by. The 111-page book was free to any bushman who wanted one, and John hoped it would be well received.

The project had taken up a large portion of John's time—time he should have been devoting to his studies. Now that *The Bushman's Companion* was published, John turned his energy and focus back to studying in the hope that he would pass his final exams. Even while he was trying to catch up on his studies, his mind was never far from thinking about the outback. He realized that if he wanted to see the mission grow to cover the whole of the outback, he needed to gather facts about the medical and spiritual needs of "the land beyond the last fence," as he referred to the enormous region, and assess how those needs were currently being met.

To travel and undertake such research, John would need money. He knew that Rosetta had just raised funds for hospital work in Korea by calling upon readers of the *Messenger* to donate enough pennies to form a line of pennies a quarter of a mile long. *Why not do the same to pay for a survey of the outback,*

John asked himself, *but instead of pennies, why not threepenny pieces?* John reasoned that threepenny pieces were much smaller than pennies. One penny was the same width as three threepenny pieces, making a line of threepenny pieces worth nine times more than a line of pennies. Altogether, he figured, a quarter-mile line of threepenny pieces would be worth 350 pounds, just enough to cover the cost of the research he wanted to do.

This was the kind of challenge John knew that people could get behind. He also knew that his name had appeared a lot in the *Messenger* recently. He asked Esther to spearhead the start of the campaign by anonymously writing to Cousin Charlotte (John's sister) and asking her to stir up the readers of the *Messenger* with the needs of isolated Australians.

John needn't have worried about his studies, or about how *The Bushman's Companion* would be received. Once again he scraped through with combined grades that got him a pass. To his relief, John had earned his divinity degree. And *The Bushman's Companion* was so well received that the initial six thousand copies printed were soon all distributed and four thousand more copies had to be printed. John began receiving letters from as far away as the Northern Territory thanking him for the book.

By mid-January 1911 John was ready to begin the next chapter in his life. The plan he concocted with Esther had worked, and a campaign to raise money for research into the nature of the inland Australia mission field had just gotten under way. On

January 20, John boarded the Adelaide Express train in Melbourne to begin his journey to Beltana. He was now thirty years of age and excited to face the future.

His first stop was Adelaide in South Australia, where he spent the first ten days of his new venture with the Reverend Robert Mitchell at the manse of the Goodwood Presbyterian Church. Robert had served as the first Smith of Dunesk missioner and, as John soon learned, had had astonishing fortitude. In the four years he was stationed at Beltana, from 1894 to 1898, he had traveled an average of three thousand miles by train and nearly as many by buggy. Each year he visited thirteen hundred homes, huts, or tents and held two hundred church services. This was a daunting achievement to follow. Robert's daughter had accompanied him on most of the buggy trips. She traveled with a portable organ that she played for people in the outback. Robert added that it was the only music some of those they visited had ever heard.

Robert went on to explain to John that one of the subsequent Smith of Dunesk missioners, Frank Rolland, who served from 1905 to 1908, had been appalled at the lack of medical help available to those living in the outback. Frank had persuaded the mission to pay for a nurse, who was now stationed at Oodnadatta, the end of the railway line that passed through Beltana.

While in Adelaide, on January 24, 1911, John was ordained as a minister in the Presbyterian Church. He was now officially the Reverend John Flynn.

On the last day of January, John boarded the train north to Beltana with Ernest Baldwin. John was too excited to stop looking out the window for the entire 350-mile journey. The farther inland the train traveled, the drier the landscape became, until the green grass that John was so used to was left behind completely.

"The gibber plain," Ernest said. "*Gibber* is the Aboriginal word for stone, so it's the stony plain or desert. It's what's left when the sand and dust are blown away by the winds. The blowing sand polishes the stones into a smooth, hard gravel. That's what you're seeing. The surface is hard now, but wait till a rain. Then it'll be all spongy."

John nodded and looked at the dry landscape studded with patches of blue-gray saltbush. Hardly a tree or any other bush was in sight. The only thing that seemed to thrive in the extreme heat and dryness was kangaroos.

The train pulled into Beltana, with its sixty cobbled-together houses, a store, and a ramshackle building that was labeled "Hotel." People waved and smiled as the train pulled to a halt.

"It's the only train on the track," Ernest noted, "and it comes only once every two weeks. I've missed it sometimes when I've been up the line, and then it's another fortnight before I can get back."

"I'll keep that in mind," John laughed as he pulled his luggage from the overhead rack and climbed down from the train.

"Welcome back, Padre. We missed you," the stationmaster said, standing on the open platform.

"Thank you," Ernest replied. "Good to see you too, Jack. How's that boy of yours?"

"Right as rain, growing like a weed," Jack said.

"I'll be over to see for myself tomorrow," Ernest replied.

John was impressed with the rapport Ernest had developed with the residents of Beltana. He hoped that as the new missioner, he would be able to do the same.

Soon the two men were standing in front of the manse, John's new home. Made of mud bricks with shutters instead of glass in the windows, and with much of the woodwork ant-eaten, it was as dilapidated as the houses around it. The two horses, Robin and Dodger, in the barn at the back were glad to see Ernest again. Ernest then set to showing John how to load up the buggy. This was serious business. The buggy had to carry not only everything John would need to keep himself alive while traveling in the outback but also his camera and photographic equipment, his magic lantern and slide shows, and a supply of *The Bushman's Companion*.

After he had oriented John to his new mission and introduced him to the residents of Beltana, Ernest returned to Adelaide, leaving John alone. Soon John was out and about. The buggy allowed him to roam the countryside, visiting huts and mining sites. He would also travel by train, stopping at many of the tiny towns along the way to hold church services. The average congregation was usually eight people, but John did not mind. This was what he had come to do. As he traveled, John always dressed immaculately in a three-piece suit with a starched white shirt and tie. The finishing touch was a gold watch and chain his father had given him. Tucked in his breast pocket was the locket with his mother's photo in it. Although the temperature soared to well above 100 degrees Fahrenheit, John felt it important to dress well as an ambassador for Christ.

On one of his journeys, John rode the train 290 miles north to the end of the railway line at Oodnadatta. This was where the Smith of Dunesk Mission's only nurse, Latto Bett, was stationed. John liked her from the moment they met. Nurse Bett was a dynamo who did her best to take care of the medical needs of the settlers spread across a huge area. The locals called her the Little White Angel of the North.

After filling John in on the realities and hardships of life in that part of the country, Latto told him, "I'm sure you've heard that we did have plans for a nursing home* a year or two ago. In fact, I believe we still have about two hundred pounds in an account for that purpose."

"Why didn't it go ahead?" John asked. "It seems like a nursing home would be a wonderful advance out here."

"It got complicated," Latto said. "Some on the committee wanted the government to cosponsor it,

---

* In Australia at the time, this was the name given to a small facility staffed and run by nurses where the medical needs of the surrounding community were tended, and where emergency treatment could be given.

but the government had rules and regulations that the committee didn't want to be bound by. It all ground to a halt, which is a pity because a nursing home is sorely needed. Currently I nurse seriously ill people in their homes—or shacks—but I don't have the equipment I need. If the people are infectious, there's no way to isolate them from everyone else in the home."

John's mind was already spinning with ideas. He decided that as he traveled around his new parish, he would keep his ears open for what people thought about having a nursing home in Oodnadatta.

News got around quickly, and wherever he went, John was instantly recognized as the padre. Not only did he travel by train and buggy during his trips, but he also traveled on an entirely different form of transport—a camel. During the nineteenth century, camels had been introduced into Australia from Arabia, India, and Afghanistan as a form of transport in the outback. They had proven to be effective at moving both people and goods across the Australian desert. John first experienced traveling on a camel during a seven-day excursion with the Government Water Conservation officer. On another occasion he accompanied expert tracker Lou Reese north on a camel, all the way up the Birdsville Track to Birdsville in southwestern Queensland and back, a nearly 750-mile round trip across the desert. On these trips John discovered that camels were not the comfiest creatures to ride on. And despite the fact that camels could walk steadily for days under the blazing desert sun, they did not walk very fast, just a little over two miles per hour, making the slow camel trips excruciatingly tedious.

In his new position as the Smith of Dunesk missionary, one thing was for sure: John was kept very busy. Yet he managed to find time to take and develop photographs and write a three-page newsletter to keep everyone informed about what he was up to and to connect the people of the outback with each other. The first issue of the newsletter, called *The Outback Battler*, was published on April 1, 1911. In introducing the newsletter John wrote, "We seek to promote [people's] well-being in matters social, educational, medical and religious." The newsletter included a report from John, an update from Nurse Bett about her work at Oodnadatta, and a record of births, deaths, and marriages throughout the district. It also carried news from the Mailbag League and included a children's section. John invited the children to send their Sunday "homework" to him in return for a reward for trying their hardest.

As he traveled and talked to the residents of the outback, John realized the dire need for not just a nursing home at Oodnadatta but also a building that housed a Christian community center in which men, women, and children could get medical, social, and spiritual help. John imagined a facility with a nursing wing and a community wing for musical concerts and lectures, a game room, and a library. The community room could also host Sunday school and church services, funerals, and weddings.

John could see that it was a tall order to think that he could resurrect the nursing home project in his first year out of college. Still, as he continued to plan the facility, he would repeat to himself the verse "With God all things are possible." The first obstacle to be overcome was money. Although they already had two hundred pounds in the bank for the project, they needed six hundred pounds more. Amazingly, someone from South Australia anonymously donated the entire amount of money needed. John took this as God's blessing on the project, which he threw his weight behind.

With the money in hand, John traveled south to Port Augusta and then on to Adelaide to have a nursing home designed. He took the plans and arranged for a builder in Port Augusta to construct the building and then ship it in pieces by train to Oodnadatta, where John would oversee its erection.

On Sunday, December 10, 1911, John stood at the door of the new nursing home and community center for the official opening of the building. Beside him stood the Reverend Robert Mitchell, who had traveled up from Adelaide for the opening ceremony. The new facility was to be called Roland House. As he looked it over, Robert declared, "This hospital is a beacon of hope, a silent ambassador for Christ in this community."

As the time approached for the official opening ceremony to begin, a massive thunderstorm broke over Oodnadatta. Lightning sliced across the sky, the wind howled, and rain pelted down, but this did not deter a large group of locals from assembling. The people stood in the rain and watched as the nursing home was dedicated and officially opened.

Even as John stood at the nursing home door for the opening, his mind was already drifting far away. He wondered how many nursing homes and community centers it would take for everyone in the outback to be no more than three hundred miles from such a facility. Eight, ten, twelve? John wasn't sure, but he had a strange confidence that he would find out for himself one day.

Chapter 6

An Urgent Call, a Noble Vision

Six months after the opening of the nursing home at Oodnadatta, John stood on the deck of the SS *Taiyuan*, watching Brisbane fade from view. He was on a ten-day voyage to Darwin, at the top of Australia. The ship, operated by the Australian Oriental Line, sailed between Sydney and Hong Kong, making stops at various ports along the way. As they headed out to sea, John thought about how much easier it was to travel around Australia by sea than overland. Even though it was 1,350 miles directly overland from Beltana to Darwin, it was much faster and less dangerous to get there by taking a train to Brisbane, making stops at Adelaide, Melbourne, and Sydney along the way, and boarding the ship for the 2,400-mile trip up the Queensland coast, around Cape York Peninsula, and on to Darwin.

The huge distances in the outback and the difficulty in covering them often led to life-or-death struggles. John thought back to his last visit to Oodnadatta. Nurse Bett had told several harrowing stories. An injured miner had been taken to the nursing home in a buggy. The trip took three weeks, during which the miner was in such excruciating pain that he could not be moved from the buggy. The injured man survived his ordeal, thanks to Nurse Bett's care. After the miner had spent ten days at the nursing home, Nurse Bett sent him five hundred miles south by train to Port Augusta for more medical treatment at the hospital there. Another incident involved a sick man who had arrived from across the desert clinging to his camel. For days he had struggled to stay alive and on his camel as he battled forward through 120-degree Fahrenheit temperatures. With Nurse Bett's care, he too had survived his illness.

John was on his way to Darwin at the request of the Federal Home Mission Board of the Presbyterian Church. The board had asked him to study the needs of the people there, the religious state of the territory, and how the Presbyterian Church could help address those needs. John had worked hard to get to this point, convincing Esther to approach Rosetta to set up a collection challenge to fund a survey of the north. Now that he was on the ship headed for the Northern Territory, he felt strangely deflated. It seemed like such an enormous task to bring help and hope to people living in an area that covered so much of Australia. He wondered what he'd been thinking. Did other people take him seriously, or did they think him ridiculous? Was his dream impossible? Laughable? John didn't know. He hoped to find an answer during this two-month trip to the Northern Territory. The *Taiyuan* made stops at Townsville, Cairns, and Thursday Island before arriving in Darwin. At each of the stops John went ashore to talk to any Christian leaders he could find.

Upon arrival in Darwin, with no time to waste, John went straight to work. He interviewed local government officials about the needs of the Northern Territory. He talked to business and civic leaders. He traveled inland to Pine Creek and Katherine, where he questioned settlers, drovers, and stockmen. He traveled up the Adelaide River, talking to people and taking notes at every stop. He also took a boat to Bathurst Island and talked with Father Gsell, who ran the Roman Catholic mission there.

John considered the highlight of his trip to the Northern Territory to be his chance to finally meet Jessie Litchfield. It was while he was reading her letter and was still a student at Ormond College that his eyes had been opened to the needs of the pioneers in inland Australia. Jessie provided John with detailed information about the local medical problems. She explained that recent outbreaks of malaria had led to the deaths of many people simply because of a lack of any medical facility to treat their illness. She told John that she'd heard about the small nursing home he had built in Oodnadatta and spoke of the need for such nursing homes in the Northern Territory.

In what seemed like no time at all, John's research trip was over, and he boarded a ship for the return journey to Sydney. On the voyage back, he was kept busy compiling a report on his findings. He called the report, which consisted of notes, photographs, and maps, *Northern Territory and Central Australia—A Call to the Church.*

As he sailed southward down the coast of Queensland, John wrote about what he had seen in the Northern Territory—the vast sheep stations, the mining prospectors, and the limitations of local governments to meet needs. He also wrote about the people he had met and the tremendous distances they had to travel to get supplies and help. He thought about the woman who had ridden on horseback for seven hours to see her closest female neighbor simply because she had not seen another white woman for a year and a half and couldn't stand the isolation any longer.

John added into the report the many things he had learned while traveling in the outback as the Smith of Dunesk missionary. As he wrote, his faith grew. John could see it all, a network of padres patrolling the outback as he had from Beltana, carrying out a pastoral and evangelistic ministry. He also suggested that a series of nursing homes modeled on the one at Oodnadatta be established so that ultimately the pioneers living in the inland would be no more than three hundred miles from competent medical care.

As he wrote his report and made his recommendations, John hoped that the photographs he had taken of conditions in the outback would help bring alive the stories he related to the Federal Home Mission Board of the Presbyterian Church. The upcoming Federal General Assembly of the Presbyterian Church was to be held in Sydney in September 1912. He knew that some of the delegates would object to his proposed two-handed approach to proclaiming the gospel—offering medical as well as spiritual care. Yet John was encouraged by reading and rereading some of the books by his missionary hero, Wilfred Grenfell. Dr. Grenfell worked with the rough-and-tumble men and women living along the Labrador Coast of Newfoundland, Canada. "When you set out to commend the Gospel to men who do not particularly want it, there is only one way to go about it—do something for them that they will be sure to understand," Dr. Grenfell had written. That was exactly what John was proposing the Presbyterian Church do, and he included the quote in his report.

John estimated that the entire plan would cost about five thousand pounds a year. That was a lot of money. It had been hard enough to collect the money to cover the cost of his research trip from the readers of the *Messenger* in Victoria. There had to be a better way to keep the money coming in year after year. Then inspiration struck John. Why not ask five thousand Christians to become the Bush Brigade. These people would each pledge to contribute one pound a year to the program. Then John would have to raise the money only once, and the giving would be ongoing. With that settled in his mind, John wrote the conclusion to his report, ending with, "Do not pray for tasks equal to your powers. Pray for powers equal to your tasks!"

The report was greeted with enthusiasm by John Ferguson, convener of the Federal Home Mission Board. "This report is not a mere document. It is a living message, an urgent call, a noble vision of Christian enterprise," he told John. Not only that, but he also agreed to publish the report, including all of John's photographs and maps, separately from the "white book" of other reports being assembled for the upcoming conference. John was delighted. This meant that his report would get much more exposure than if it were just one of many reports in the stodgy white book.

On the morning of September 26, 1912, John looked out over the top of his glasses at the assembled delegates, before pushing his glasses high on the bridge of his nose and launching into his presentation. On an easel beside him was a large map of Australia. John was nervous at first but soon felt himself relax as the details and recommendations of his report began to flow freely. At times he would point to various areas on the map beside him as he spoke.

John's presentation seemed to resonate with the delegates attending the Presbyterian Church's General Assembly, and on the last day of the conference they voted to approve John's recommendation. They gave him a two-year appointment as the organizing agent and superintendent of a special home mission region that would include the Northern Territory and adjacent areas. They also decided that the new organization overseeing this region would be called the Australian Inland Mission, AIM for short, though many of the delegates were already referring to it as the Bush Department. John now had a job title, a 250-pounds-per-year stipend, and two years to prove that he could turn his dream into a reality. John and the Australian Inland Mission would operate under the oversight of the Federal Home Mission Board.

John's first task was to find a person to replace him at Beltana. This proved to be discouraging. No matter how many church services and meetings he spoke at, John could not interest any Presbyterian pastor to volunteer to take over in Beltana. Without the right men and women in the new mission field, there would be no way forward. One man, twenty-five-year-old Robert Plowman, who was known by his middle name Bruce, did seek John out after one of his meetings to express his interest in taking up the position. However, he was not an ordained minister, which the Home Mission Board required. Still, John offered to put Bruce's name forward for the position. He organized a meeting with him and several members of the Home Mission Board. The meeting did not go well until the treasurer asked Bruce a strange question: "How many senses are there?"

Bruce thought for a minute and then grinned. "Six," he replied.

"What's the sixth?" the treasurer asked.

"Horse sense, or common sense," Bruce answered.

The board members laughed.

"Well," the treasurer said, "let's hope you have plenty of that. I think you'll do."

The other board members agreed, and Bruce was sent off to replace John as the padre at Beltana.

With his replacement found, the next year was busy for John. He traveled around the south and east coasts of Australia getting the message out about the new mission and seeking people who would commit to become one of the five thousand Bush Brigade members to help fund the new venture year by year. He also recruited and appointed two new padres, Jim Stevens and Frank Brady, who would be based in Western Australia, one at Broome and the other at Port Hedland.

In early 1913 John got to do the thing he wanted to do most of all—head back into the inland to see conditions firsthand. In particular, he wanted to travel to Alice Springs in the Northern Territory. From Oodnadatta he traveled north by stagecoach to Horseshoe Bend, where the road ended. From there he arranged to travel on with Texas, the colorful mailman, and his string of camels.

The men set off north across the desert under a bright blue sky. The scenery was monotonous— just red sand for miles in every direction broken by clumps of spinifex and the occasional desert oak tree. Texas rode the lead camel. The second camel, attached by a rope from the first camel's tail to its nose plug, carried bags of mail. The third camel, attached to the camel in front in the same way, was loaded with canteens of water, food, cooking utensils, and several bags. Sitting on top of this camel was Pup, Texas's dog. The fourth camel carried their swags, blankets, more water canteens, and John.

At night the men would camp beside the trail. After they had cooked and eaten their dinner, they would sit by the fire and drink tea and talk. Texas told John that he was from the United States. John had already guessed that from his accent. Texas had been a cowboy, driving great herds of cattle to market. He had drifted up to northwestern Canada, where he joined the Mounted Police. One winter, while on patrol as a Mountie, he had suffered frostbite, which is why he now walked with a limp. From Canada, Texas had made his way to Australia, where he was now content to carry His Majesty's mail across the outback by camel. He loved to read, and given the slow pace of the camels and the fact that they knew the trail so well, Texas was able to get a lot of reading in each day. John had noticed the way Texas hunched over on his camel, rested a book on the creature's hump, and read for hours on end, almost oblivious to where he was. John, on the other hand, was too interested in the land, as monotonous as it was, that they were passing through.

Alice Springs lay in a natural amphitheater in the MacDonnell Ranges, almost at the geographic center of Australia. The nearest town to the south was four hundred miles away, and the nearest to the north was eight hundred miles away. As John looked down at

Alice Springs from his camel, the place turned out to be smaller than he had imagined it to be. It consisted of a few homes scattered around a hotel, two shops, and a police outpost. The place was hot and dusty. It was also one of the places John had noted in his report to the General Assembly where AIM should build a nursing home.

Captivated by the blue, white, purple, orange, and red colors of the mountains of the MacDonnell Ranges, particularly Mount Gillen, John spent time hiking around and through the mountains taking photographs. He also spent time talking to the local population, almost entirely men, about establishing a nursing home in their community. Most thought it was a good idea and told him so. But then almost every man he spoke to added, "But what about the nurses, Padre? This is no place for women."

John had heard this sentiment repeated many times by men in the outback and knew exactly how to reply. "Then we must change that," he said. "In the long run, country that is not fit for women is not fit for men either."

All too soon it was time to climb back onto his camel and leave the isolation of Alice Springs behind. As he headed back south, John thought about his visit. Texas had been right. He had told John on the way to Alice Springs that the people there, mostly water well drillers and stockmen, were among the most independent men he would ever meet. Yet they had embraced the idea of a nursing home in their community but were concerned about the nurses living in such a harsh environment.

John was well aware that a place like Alice Springs, or Oodnadatta, for that matter, was no place for women. Yet he knew that if life in the outback was to change for the better, it needed to become a place for women. And to become a place for women, one of the necessities was easy access to medical care and a place where women could give birth to their babies and sick children could be taken care of. Until then, most women would not risk pioneering alongside men in the outback. John knew that was why nursing homes were so vital in the outlying communities. Once they were established, he was sure that churches and Sunday schools would follow.

Chapter 7

Challenges

Traveling back from Alice Springs, John thought of his early schooling. He'd always enjoyed studying geography, yet in all the geography classes he took in school he had learned almost nothing about the interior of Australia. Why was that? As he swayed back and forth atop his camel, he concluded that it was because very little was published about the outback. By the time John reached the end of his journey, a plan had formed in his mind to help right that situation. He could see it already: a quality magazine of maybe fifty pages that would contain information about inland Australia, the nature of the landscape and people living there, and the work of AIM in the outback. The magazine would be aimed at both those living in the inland and the other Australians who lived in the towns and cities of the coastal region. It would be available in public libraries and could be bought in local bookshops and at newsstands. The ambitious vision would cost a lot of money, but John was sure it was the next step for the Australian Inland Mission.

The AIM board did not share John's enthusiasm, however. When he presented the idea for the magazine, to be called the *Inlander*, to board members, they voted the project down. By now, enthusiasm for John's ideas was dwindling among many Presbyterians and being replaced by growing concern about the state of tension slowly building in Europe.

Despite the board's initial rejection, John was not ready to give up on his idea. He was sure that a high-quality magazine would carry the vision of AIM across the country. John's vision was not on Europe or anywhere else. Because it was focused solely on inland Australia, his mission field, eventually he wore the board down. They agreed to let him work on the magazine but with almost no budget to cover its costs. John set to work traveling and selling the idea of the magazine to everyone he spoke to and collecting material to include in the publication. The first issue of the *Inlander* was all he'd hoped it would be—glossy, professional, and well received. It was published just before Christmas 1913. John was happy with the result.

Besides overseeing the new magazine and the ongoing ministry of AIM, John continued to travel the country describing the vision of the ministry and trying to raise more financial support for it. He was delighted now to have copies of the *Inlander* to give to those interested in the work of AIM.

In early 1914 John made a four-month trip to Western Australia. He was anxious to check on the ministry of the AIM patrol padres in Broome and Port Hedland and assess future ministry opportunities there. John spent part of the trip traveling with patrol padre Jim Stevens, who worked out of Port Hedland. Once again John was happy to be traveling in the outback, going from small community to small community holding church services and ministering and preaching the gospel. Traveling also gave him the opportunity to talk to the locals and learn how much they depended upon Jim's visits for support and encouragement in the isolated backcountry.

John was regularly receiving letters from Bruce Plowman reporting on his patrol padre work in South Australia. Bruce had moved his base of operations from Beltana to Oodnadatta, where he kept busy traveling by camel, making visits to the outlying communities and cattle stations.

Back in Sydney, where the AIM office was located on York Street, John began preparing a detailed report of the work of AIM to be presented at the next Federal General Assembly of the Presbyterian Church. On August 4, 1914, as he was putting the finishing touches on his report, war broke out, with Great Britain and France pitted against Germany and the Austro-Hungarian Empire. As soon as news of the war in Europe reached Australia, Prime Minister

Joseph Cook pledged the nation's full military support for Great Britain. Almost immediately troops were raised and sent from Australia to Europe to fight, creating in the country a shortage of young men, including Christian ministers, many of whom volunteered to go as army chaplains.

John realized that it was not a good time to be talking about raising money for projects in the inland, but in September he delivered his report to the Federal General Assembly. The report was a mixed bag. There were now three ordained and one lay patrol padres, a nurse at Oodnadatta, and John serving with AIM. Money to support their mission, however, was not coming in as hoped. John had called for five thousand pounds from his Bush Brigade, but less than half that amount had been collected thus far. Still, as John addressed the delegates, he assured them that he had a new plan. He recommended that the Australian Inland Mission divide the inland into ten patrol areas, each with a patrol padre. He also recommended that within the next ten years the mission should recruit fifteen more ordained pastors and four more nurses and erect twenty buildings.

When he was asked how much this would cost, he had the figure ready: 10,650 pounds. The delegates stared at John in stunned silence. Was that really possible? Shouldn't AIM concentrate on the areas they were already working in? John could see the concern on the faces of the delegates, and he reminded them of the closing line of his report two years before: "Do not pray for tasks equal to your powers. Pray for powers equal to your tasks." It took a lot of talking, but John won over the delegates, who agreed to reappoint him as the superintendent of AIM for another two years. John was now faced with the tremendous challenge of keeping the eyes of Australians on the needs of the inland while the country was busy sending many of its brightest young men off to fight in Europe.

As he thought about the ministry of AIM going forward with so many Australian men being sent away to fight, John decided to switch the emphasis from patrol padres to nurses. Jim Stevens, the patrol padre from Port Hedland, had already signed up for the war effort and was en route to Europe, as was Nurse Bett from Oodnadatta.

Not only were personnel in short supply, but also money to fund the mission was drying up. This was because many Australian families, with a father or husband away fighting in the war, were trying to put food on the table. John carried on as best he could, encouraging his remaining patrol padres. He continued to speak at churches all over the country about the ongoing work of the Australian Inland Mission.

One year after the General Assembly of 1914, John was totally exhausted. While forging ahead with the ministry of AIM, he was buried under a mountain of office work. He knew it was important to keep up with all the paperwork, but to him it was busywork that sapped his time and energy. What he really needed was a private secretary. He'd asked at the previous General Assembly that one be appointed to help him, but there had been no money in the budget for such a luxury. Instead, as John prayed about the paperwork situation in the AIM office, an entirely different solution occurred to him. If he could not have one full-time secretary, why not have ten or even twenty part-time volunteer office workers? They could work as a team, like the Mailbag League, where the women worked together to efficiently mail out hundreds of pounds of books and magazines to the outback each month. What if he could find dedicated people who would spare a night a week to help share the load of AIM office work?

John's first office team, or OT, as he called it, began in the AIM office in Sydney on a Thursday night. On the first night seven men and women showed up to do what they could to help organize the mission's paperwork and make John's role easier. The approach worked. Soon other OT groups were meeting at the office on different nights, until there was one OT group for every night of the week. At last John felt free to continue pushing for the expansion of AIM nursing homes into new areas of inland Australia.

In 1915 John declared that AIM would build a nursing home at Port Hedland. Gold had been discovered in the area, and the Pilbarra goldfields were among the most dangerous in the world because of the extremely hot temperatures of the region. At first it was difficult to find staff for the new venture. Over twenty nurses who had expressed an interest in serving with AIM had left the country to help with the war effort in Europe. Eventually a suitable nurse was found, and the nursing home, modeled on the one in Oodnadatta, was opened.

Despite the war effort and the shortage of men, John managed to recruit two more pastors to serve as patrol padres. Frank Heriot began a new patrol padre circuit based out of Cloncurry in Queensland, and Jim Gibson worked a new circuit based out of Pine Creek in the Northern Territory.

With the Port Hedland nursing home successfully up and running, John received an urgent telegram from patrol padre Jim Gibson asking if a nurse could be sent to help with a malaria outbreak in Maranboy, a tin-mining shantytown in the Northern Territory. Already hundreds of men in the area had succumbed to malaria. Jim wondered if a nursing home could be established in the area. The surviving residents of Maranboy were eager to have one and had already taken up a collection to raise money to cover some of the cost. Seeing an opportunity, John got right to work. He negotiated with the government of the Northern Territory, which agreed to pay to have a facility built at Maranboy according to John's specifications. AIM would provide the staff to run it. Soon the nursing home at Maranboy was opened and fully staffed.

Before dispatching Nurse Hepburn and her assistant, May Gillespie, to Maranboy, John gave them their job instructions. Besides giving medical treatment, they were also, as part of their job, to improve the general hygiene and diet of the men in the settlement. John also reminded the nurses that as Christians they were to minister to the whole man. He told them that it does no good to mend a man's physical wounds if the man remains wounded in his spirit. It was part of the women's ministry to engage the men in conversation and discuss their spiritual condition, pointing the way to Jesus Christ to heal the inner man.

As more men were called up and sent to fight in Europe, John did what he could for the war effort, including collecting funds for the Red Cross wherever he went. He noticed at his meetings that people gave twice as much to the Red Cross as they did to AIM. He understood why. People knew the nature of war and how soldiers got wounded and needed help, but it was difficult for urban dwellers to grasp the remote and hostile nature of the environment in which pioneers lived in the outback. But in early September 1917 something happened that changed all that.

One day when John arrived at his office in Sydney, a member of the office team asked, "Have you seen today's paper, Mr. Flynn?"

"No," John replied. "Is there something in it I should know about? Something about the war?"

"No, much closer to home," the man said, handing John a copy of the newspaper. "I think you'll be interested in the story on the front page."

As John scanned the newspaper, his eyes fell on the headline: "Mad Dash to Save Fallen Man Fails." John sat down at his desk and began to read the long article that reported the story of a young man named Jimmy Darcy, a stockman at Ruby Plains homestead in the Kimberley region of northern Western Australia. In the early hours of July 28, 1917, Jimmy had fallen from his horse when the animal stopped suddenly. Jimmy was seriously injured, was in great pain, and needed urgent medical care. Two of his friends gently loaded him onto a springless buggy and set off for the hamlet of Hall's Creek, forty-seven miles away. The journey took them twelve hours, as they made constant stops along the way when the pain of bumping along in the buggy became too much for Jimmy.

The men reached Hall's Creek at 2:00 a.m. and pulled up in front of the telegraph station run by Fred Tuckett, rousing him from sleep. Fred, like John, had completed the St. John's first aid course and was competent at tending to minor injuries. However, Jimmy's injuries went way beyond Fred's medical knowledge and ability. Fred gave Jimmy some morphine for his pain. Then by telegraph he contacted Wyndham, 250 miles away to the north, and Derby, 450 miles to the west, where the two closest doctors were located. Neither doctor was available. Fred needed help with his diagnosis, and he telegraphed Dr. John Holland in Perth. Dr. Holland had been his instructor for the St. John's first aid course. Perth was 1,250 miles away to the southwest in a direct line overland from Hall's Creek. However, the messages telegraphed back and forth between Fred and Dr. Holland were relayed along 2,283 miles of telegraph wire that followed the coastline of Western Australia.

Back and forth went the telegrams, with Fred describing Jimmy's symptoms. Dr. Holland would telegraph questions, and Fred would answer them until the doctor had made a diagnosis: Jimmy had a ruptured bladder. But there was a surprise in the telegram from Dr. Holland. "You must operate on him at once."

"I'm not a surgeon, and I have no scalpel," Fred telegraphed back.

"If you don't operate, he will die. You have a penknife or a razor, don't you?" came the response.

Fred had no better option. Dr. Holland sent detailed instructions while Fred had Jimmy lashed to the table. There was no anesthetic, and Fred had to work by the light of an oil lamp as he took his penknife and began the surgery. Jimmy's two friends were instructed to hold him down and try to keep the flies away as Fred operated. Fred succeeded in mending Jimmy's ruptured bladder. He took a deep breath and sewed the incision closed.

At first Jimmy's condition stabilized, but then it began to deteriorate. After more consultations by telegraph with Dr. Holland in Perth, Fred had to perform another surgery on his patient in the afternoon.

In the meantime, Dr. Holland decided to set out for Hall's Creek to check on Jimmy firsthand. There was no direct route from Perth to Hall's Creek. Dr. Holland took a cattle boat north up the coast to Derby, a six-day journey. He was frustrated when the boat had to anchor for twelve hours awaiting the right tide to enter the harbor. From Derby Dr. Holland was driven over a rough track in a Ford Model T to Fitzroy Crossing, 250 miles inland. At Fitzroy Crossing he changed to a smaller car that could better handle the even rougher terrain on the last leg of the journey. But the car repeatedly broke down, costing the doctor thirty-six hours while various repairs were made.

One breakdown was repaired by cutting a section of rubber tubing from the doctor's stethoscope that was then used to feed gasoline directly into the carburetor. Eventually the car engine gave out completely. The doctor walked back to the nearest cattle station, where an Aborigine boy caught two horses and hitched them to a sulky for the remainder of the journey. Twelve and a half days after setting out from Perth, Dr. Holland arrived in Hall's Creek. The doctor introduced himself to Fred Tuckett and asked how the patient was.

"He died yesterday," Fred replied.

Dejected, Dr. Holland walked inside to examine Jimmy's body. After performing an autopsy, the doctor announced that Jimmy had died from malaria and not from complications of Fred's surgeries. In fact, he was impressed with Fred's surgical skills and the job he had done under such difficult circumstances.

When he had finished reading the entire article, John took a deep breath, stabbed at the newspaper with his finger, and said to those working around him, "That's why we need our nursing homes. But we need so much more. Distance is the enemy in the outback. It takes so long to get anywhere. There has to be a faster way to get sick people out for proper medical help."

News of Jimmy Darcy's harrowing story captivated the nation, pushing headlines about progress
in the war off the front page. Over the next several weeks, John spoke to groups about Jimmy's
death. He was amazed at how many people had
been touched by the story. Many Australians were
genuinely shocked to learn of the primitive conditions that existed in the outback of their own country. They were beginning to understand for the first
time the challenges present in their "backyard." John
also used the opportunity to write an article for the
Inlander about what had happened at Hall's Creek.

Several months after the tragedy at Hall's Creek,
John received a letter from Fred Tuckett. Fred
explained that the manager of Mullabulla station had
met John in Sydney on a trip and been impressed by
him. The station manager had told Fred about the
work of the Australian Inland Mission. In turn, Fred,
who was influential in the community, had called a
meeting of locals to talk about setting up a medical
facility. At the meeting the people even collected two
hundred pounds in donations toward the project and
agreed to make the Hall's Creek Miner's Institute
Hall available to serve as a temporary nursing home.
Fred asked John if AIM could provide a trained nurse
and a helper, along with the necessary equipment
and supplies to set up and run the nursing home.

Even though he knew it would not be easy, given
how stretched the mission's resources were, John
promised that he would do everything he could to
establish an AIM nursing home at Hall's Creek. The

community surely needed such a facility. But so did many other tiny towns dotted across the Australian outback. As John stared at a map of the country in his Sydney office, he wondered how he would ever raise enough money and recruit enough staff to bring physical and spiritual help to all who needed it. It seemed an impossible dream, yet one that he refused to give up.

Chapter 8

Mantle of Safety

The war and long patrols through the outback took their toll on the padres. During 1917, Bruce Plowman, patrol padre for the Central Patrol based out of Oodnadatta, suffered a nervous breakdown during one of his patrols. John insisted on traveling inland to escort Bruce home to the coast to recover. Jim Stevens, patrol padre at Port Hedland, Western Australia, had volunteered to serve in the war and planned on returning to the position after the war. But Jim was killed fighting in Europe. John was devastated by both events. AIM needed to regroup, and John prayed that more men would come forward and commit themselves to serving as patrol padres. However, Christian ministers of all types were in short supply.

Shortly after Bruce's nervous breakdown, John was speaking at an AIM rally in the Presbyterian church on Phillip Street in Sydney. A young man approached him following the service. He introduced himself as Kingsley Partridge, and he looked familiar to John. Kingsley said they had met and spent time talking together four years before in Tasmania, where he had been attending college. He told John he'd been deeply stirred by their conversation. Kingsley had graduated and was now ordained. In fact, he'd done so well academically he had earned a scholarship for further study in Scotland.

As John listened to Kingsley, he sensed that this was the man to take over as padre for the Central Patrol. When John told him of the opening, Kingsley refused the position. "What about my academic future?" he asked. "I'm off to Scotland for postgraduate study. I can't just drop that and head to the inland of Australia."

But John persisted. He was certain that Kingsley Partridge was his man. Kingsley finally agreed to take on the role for a short while before heading to Scotland. Before he knew it, he was on his way to Oodnadatta to replace Bruce Plowman on the Central Patrol.

Kingsley was introduced to the reality of life in the outback on his very first patrol. He recounted the event to John in a letter. He had traveled to a cattle station about seventy miles from Oodnadatta and was preparing to leave when one of the men at the station suddenly took ill. A motorcar was available at the station, and a plan was hatched to drive it to Ood-nadatta, pick up the nurse there, and bring her back to tend to the sick man. But before the car returned, the man's condition steadily worsened, and he died. As a result, Kingsley held his first burial service in the outback. Before he could officiate the funeral, he had to assist the carpenter in making a coffin and then dig the grave to put it in.

Just weeks later in another letter to John, Kingsley related an incident he'd been involved in at the small mining community of Hatch's Creek. He arrived at the ramshackle community to find that a miner, Richard Brown, had just committed suicide. Richard had apparently strained himself while working in the mine ten days before. Slowly his condition had worsened until he could take the pain no longer and shot himself. Before he could conduct the funeral and in order to meet legal requirements, Kingsley led a group of six local men, not present at the incident, in an inquiry into the miner's death. The men gathered evidence from several people who had seen a disheveled Richard standing at the door of the building he was staying at before going inside. Shortly afterward they had heard a gunshot.

Kingsley learned that in the outback, suicide was known as the bushman's way out. Rather than be a burden to his mates because of illness or some other impediment, a man would take his own life. After more evidence was collected about Richard's health and general demeanor, the inquiry committee officially ruled his death a suicide. With that out of the way, Kingsley once again helped the carpenter build a coffin and then dug a grave before he conducted Richard's funeral.

The account of the incident from Kingsley's letter disturbed John. A man was dead by his own hand because he was in an isolated outback community, too far from the nearest telegraph station from which help could have been called for and hundreds of miles from the nearest medical care. John concluded that it was the huge distances in the inland that were really killing people. Richard would most likely still be alive had there been a fast and convenient way to get him to a hospital.

In November 1917 John was still mulling the sense-less death of Richard Brown at Hatch's Creek. He received a long letter from a young medical student aboard a troopship on his way to the war in Europe. Clifford Peel was from Inverleigh, Victoria, and was a member of the new Australian Flying Corps. In his letter, which he had given the title *A Young Austra-lian's Vision—Aeroplanes for the Inland*, Clifford dis-cussed the use of airplanes in the outback. He began by saying, "Aviation is still new, but it has set some of us thinking, and thinking hard. Perhaps others want to be thinking too. Hence these few words."

For several years John had wondered about using airplanes in the outback. Because flying was so new and many early flying machines had proven unreli-able, leading to deadly crashes, he had not pursued the idea. John thought that might be about to change as he sat down and eagerly began reading Clifford's letter. John was not disappointed. By the time he had finished the letter, he was filled with enthusiasm. Not only had Clifford calmed many of John's concerns about using airplanes in the outback, but also he'd laid out in detail just how to do it.

Clifford proposed that AIM own and operate four airplanes, one each to be based at Cloncurry in Queensland, Oodnadatta in South Australia, and Katherine in the Northern Territory. He chose these three locations, since they were situated at railheads, making it relatively easy to transport the fuel and equipment the planes would need to operate. These three airplanes would be used to fly the sick and injured to nursing homes or hospitals. The fourth plane would be used to ferry a doctor to isolated rural communities.

Clifford showed how, by operating out of these three locations, a good part of inland Australia would be within reach of medical care. He even provided a list of the various rural communities that could be reached from each location, detailing how long it would take an airplane flying at ninety miles per hour to reach each location and how much fuel each plane would use. He estimated that it would cost the mission eight pence a mile to fly each airplane. He also gave a figure of 10,600 pounds as the cost of purchasing the four airplanes and providing hangars in which to house them when not in use.

For under eleven thousand pounds, AIM could be operating airplanes in the Australian outback! John's imagination ran wild. Not only could they fly sick and injured people out for medical care, but also the airplanes could deliver the mail and other vital supplies. Eager to share the dream, John published Clifford's letter in the *Inlander*. Just as that issue of the magazine was going to press, he received word that Clifford had been killed in action while flying a photographic reconnaissance mission over France.

The sobering news made John more determined than ever to present Clifford's idea to the AIM board. The board just stared at John in disbelief when he put forward the proposal. "What are you thinking?" one board member asked. "We are in the middle of a war. We have rationing, people are going without, and you want to raise ten thousand pounds—over three times our yearly budget at the moment! What's wrong with you?"

"I don't care what that young man says," another board member chimed in. "Airplanes just aren't safe enough. No sick person would want to climb into one. He'd rather stay on the ground. I can guarantee that."

"Think of the expense," another commented. "We can barely stay afloat financially right now. How could we afford to service an airplane? And they'd need landing strips and refueling stations. It's just not what we are about as a mission."

John listened patiently as various board members ripped the vision to shreds. When they had exhausted themselves, he began to answer their objections. "You've all read young Peel's letter. As he points out, after the initial outlay, the airplanes will be cheap to run. The main point is not the cost but the lives saved and the isolation bridged. Doctors need wings to fly over the terrain. In the wet season there's no way through by road, and the distances cost lives. Look at Jimmy Darcy. Believe me when I say it, gentlemen. As far as the inland is concerned, it is either airplanes or coffins. I'm not exaggerating. And as for the safety issues, again Peel points out that because of their use in the war, airplanes are much more advanced and safer today than they have ever been."

The board calmed down in the face of John's response, but John could see that they were not about to give in to his proposal. As far as they were concerned, there was no money in the mission coffers to be used to explore the use of airplanes. Instead, the members of the AIM board urged John to turn his focus back to the work at hand: establishing more patrol padre circuits and setting up more nursing homes in the outback run by qualified and dedicated Christian nurses. With that, the board meeting came to an end.

John was disappointed by the outcome. The AIM board was beginning to feel less like a team and more like a weight he dragged behind him. His spirits were lifted later in the week when he received a check for one hundred pounds from a prominent banker in Singapore. The man had read Clifford Peel's letter in the *Inlander* and wanted to donate toward an airplane service to the outback. John asked for permission to set up a separate account for an aerial medical service, and the board allowed him to do so. He was one hundredth of the way toward the ten thousand pounds needed to start the project.

By the middle of 1918, Nurse Elizabeth Rogasch and her assistant, Mary Madigan, were on their way to set up and staff the new nursing home at Hall's Creek in the Kimberley region of Western Australia. Their journey to Hall's Creek took them across the country by train to Perth, where they met with John Holland. Dr. Holland related to them his firsthand account of the incident in Hall's Creek involving Jimmy Darcy. He also helped the women buy hospital supplies and home comforts to make their time in the outback a little easier.

From Perth the two women traveled north by ship to Wyndham. They were then to be escorted to Hall's Creek with their luggage and supplies. But when the ship docked in Wyndham, Elizabeth wrote John that an urgent message was waiting for them from the telegraph station at Hall's Creek. Another tragic event had taken place in the settlement. Mr. Ward, the local storekeeper and honorary secretary of the new Hall's Creek Hospital committee, had been shot and wounded by an attacker, who had then shot himself. Mr. Ward needed urgent emergency treatment. Nurse Rogasch raced by car against time the 250 miles south, bouncing over heavily rutted tracks. Mary stayed in Wyndham with their luggage. Elizabeth and her driver covered the distance to Hall's Creek in record time, and Elizabeth was able to treat the storekeeper and save his life. Mary and the luggage were then escorted to Hall's Creek, where the two women soon had the nursing home up and running. As he read Nurse Rogasch's letter, John smiled to himself. Elizabeth had certainly been given a crash course on the reality of being an AIM nurse in the outback.

John was pleased with the way AIM was growing and ministering to more and more people in the inland, despite the shortage of funds and manpower brought on by the war. More than anything, he was delighted that through the dedication of the AIM nurses and the padres, people in the outback were seeing firsthand the life-changing power of the gospel at work through acts of Christian love and caring.

AIM had also just begun work on another project that John had dreamed about and planned since his visit to Alice Springs in 1913. In his report that led to the founding of the Australian Inland Mission, John had proposed building a nursing home in Alice Springs. Work had just gotten under way there to build the structure to house the nursing home. John worked with an architect and came up with an innovative layout for the place. The building was designed to have a natural ventilation system that would both cool and filter the air entering the nursing home. To do this, a basement tunnel was constructed under the building to draw in the outside air and funnel it up through large vents into the structure. As the air passed along the tunnel, it went through staggered wet sacks kept moist by a flow of water. The sacks served to both cool the air and filter out any impurities.

A builder was now constructing the tunnel and foundation and would soon begin erecting the stone walls. John knew that it would be a grand structure when completed. He also knew that the nursing home would make a difference in the lives of the people living in the center of Australia. Yet he was also convinced that there was so much more the mission could do over time. The trouble was, waiting was the one thing John Flynn was not good at, especially when people's lives were at stake.

On November 11, 1918, the Great War in Europe came to an end with the surrender of Germany. By then, approximately sixty thousand Australian young men had been killed in the fighting. It was now time to rebuild the country and refocus on making Australia strong and prosperous. John decided that this might be the right time to appeal to the Defense Department. Surely the war had shown the country's leaders the value of air power, and they would want to continue with an Australian Air Force. And what better place to practice flying maneuvers than in the real-life situations of outback emergencies. John wrote to the minister of defense, asking him to think about partnering with AIM to put airplanes in the sky over Australia. He also pointed out that if Australia were ever invaded by a foreign force, it would probably be from Asia to their north. Wouldn't it be wise, John asked, to have an air force that could repel invasion from the north?

The response John received was less than flattering. The Defense Department treated John like a crackpot, making fun of his ideas. It was obvious to him that the Defense Department was not going to help out with his flying scheme anytime soon. But someone had to because it was going to cost a lot of money to start an aerial medical service in the inland.

Never one to give up, John decided to appeal directly to the Australian people. If he could make them see the value of an air service, his hope was that they would put pressure on the government to do something. First he set to work producing a new map of Australia, building upon Clifford Peel's proposal. The map was marked with sixteen sky doctor bases from which airplanes could cover all of inland Australia in what John was referring to as a Mantle of Safety.

With his new map in hand, John then started making the rounds of the local and national newspapers, talking to reporters and editors and describing his dream of using airplanes in the inland. Most of the newspapers wrote in support of his plan, with the *West Australian Age* saying, "The Australian Inland Mission now contemplates a ring of aerial doctors around the continent where flying radii would reach to even the most remote settlers. . . . It is not impossible. Could we but look into the mysteries that Father Time has tentatively in store for us, especially in his inventory of scientific wonders, we would chide ourselves for our hesitating lack of present belief."

The *Sydney Daily Telegraph* wrote, "It is evident that no migration into the remote parts of our inland will ever begin to any extent until the essentials of community life are within short call by means of aerial and wireless communication."

Other newspapers were just as supportive, and John began to feel that public opinion was slowly turning toward the use of aerial doctors. But still no money was available in the AIM budget for him to move forward with his plans. In 1919, however, the board did find enough money in the budget to hire Thomas Ramage to work full-time in the AIM office as John's private secretary. John was delighted. Although the office team, which came in the evenings to help him take care of the necessary paperwork, had been a great help, Thomas was even more valuable to John. He simply took over doing many of the tasks John dreaded. Having someone regularly in the office answering queries and letters and directing the office team made it easier on John when he traveled to speak in churches or to visit and encourage mission personnel in the field. John no longer dreaded returning to the office to face piles of unanswered letters, messages, and other paperwork that used to await him.

As John continued to pursue the use of airplanes in the outback, he realized that another problem would need to be addressed. Airplanes were just half of the equation. They could get a doctor out to an emergency or transport a sick or injured person to a hospital, but how would someone inform the doctor in the first place that an emergency had occurred far out in the countryside? Some areas of the inland were lucky enough to have telegraph service, but most did not. John studied the problem. How could a sheepherder or a miner's wife call for help from just anywhere in the outback? There was only one answer—the new and evolving technology of radio.

In mid-1919, John set out to learn all he could about radio transmission. He visited the armed forces and the postmaster general's office to see the latest advances. What he learned was not encouraging. Yes, there was technology to send Morse code messages long distances using radio waves, but the equipment required to do this was enormous, delicate, and complicated and cost thousands of pounds. John noted that the necessary radio equipment took up an entire room and required three operators to maintain it and send the messages. He shook his head as he left the postmaster general's office. This was not what he needed at all. What he needed was a radio that was simple, unbreakable, portable, cheap, and able to carry a voice, not Morse code, across a thousand miles. John knew what he wanted. He also knew that it did not yet exist. He just hoped that he wouldn't have to wait much longer for such a device to be made. Lives depended on it.

Chapter 9

A Frustrating Lack of Vision

With positive comments from the country's news-papers about using airplanes in the outback and regular updates in the *Inlander* about their use-fulness, the public became enthralled with the aerial medical project. But there was little acknowledgment from the Australian government about the many needs of the people living beyond the "last fence." The job of reaching across the entire inland and offer-ing the services and help these pioneers needed was so vast that the government would eventually have to become involved. But what would be the best strategy? That was the question that John pondered.

In 1920 three members of the Commonwealth Par-liament, two senators and an MP, were charged with investigating the possibility of extending the railway

line from Oodnadatta northward to Alice Springs.
John received a letter from the Reverend Coledge
Harland, the new Central Patrol padre. Coledge had
replaced Kingsley Partridge the year before, when
Kingsley departed for Scotland to do his postgraduate
study. Coledge had told John of the visit of the three
politicians, who had arrived by train in Oodnadatta.
When the men could not find a place to stay, Coledge
offered them the AIM manse. He also became their
friend and guide, accompanying the three on horseback north to Alice Springs and beyond, making it all
the way to the AIM nursing home at Maranboy.

Along the way, the men experienced firsthand the
isolation of the outback. In Alice Springs, Coledge had
pointed out the foundation and walls of what was
to have been the AIM nursing home there. The project had come to a halt when funds ran out. Coledge
noted in his letter that some of the locals now referred
to the abandoned building site as Flynn's Folly. John
smiled when he read this. *Faith may be delayed, but it
will succeed in the end. They'll see*, he said to himself.
He had not given up on the dream of a nursing home
in Alice Springs and trusted that God would allow
him to finish the building one day. Coledge reported
that after a month in the outback, the three politicians declared that they were so impressed with the
work of the Australian Inland Mission that they were
ready to do whatever it took to support it.

This was just the kind of news that John needed
to hear. Now that the public and members of the
Commonwealth Parliament were behind him, it was

time to ask some of Australia's big industrialists to join the cause. John soon found the man he was looking for: the man he'd first met as a boy out hunting rabbits on the plain beyond Braybrook—Hugh Victor McKay. McKay's Sunshine Harvester business had been hugely successful, and now McKay was far wealthier and more influential in the country than when John had first met him. He remained a staunch Presbyterian and had followed AIM's progress from the beginning. Now he had indicated that he was ready to meet with John and listen to his ideas and plans for the future.

McKay greeted John warmly and told him he still remembered the day the two first met. John told him about his plan to use airplanes in the inland to take doctors to the sick and injured and, if need be, transport them to the nearest hospital. McKay listened attentively as John described his vision and then told John that he believed that a regular airmail and passenger service would have to be working well before AIM could put its first airplane into the sky. John could see the logic of what McKay was saying, and he was prepared to wait. He knew it would be only a matter of months before this happened. And when it did, the public would become more confident in the safety of airplanes and air travel. McKay promised that he would provide AIM with the financial help it needed when the right time came to start a sky doctor service.

In late November 1921, John had another important meeting, this time with a man named Hudson

Fysh. Hudson had been a lieutenant in the Australian Flying Corps during the war, clocking five hundred hours of combat flying. Upon his return to Australia, he and his friend Paul McGinness had started the first air service in Queensland and the Northern Territory. Their two-airplane business was called Queensland and Northern Territory Aerial Services, Ltd., but most people simply referred to it as Qantas.

John and Hudson met at Sydney's Metropole Hotel, where John lived whenever he was in Sydney. John arrived at the meeting in the hotel's writing room carrying several maps under his arm. After introducing himself to Hudson, he rolled the maps out on the table between them and began plying Hudson with question after question: Were there suitable landing sites in Northern Queensland and the Northern Territory? What kind of airplane would Hudson recommend? Was it better to buy their own plane or rent one? Did Qantas have an airplane big enough to carry a patient on a stretcher? What type of communication could be used between the airplane and the ground?

Hudson patiently answered each of John's questions as best he could. He told John that he admired his vision for an aerial medical service in the outback, that Qantas and John had the same goal in mind. "We both have the same big object in view—the opening up of Australia's 'back yard,'" he said. As to an airplane that could carry a patient on a stretcher, it did not yet exist. Hudson assured John that such a plane soon would exist, as a wave of innovative aircraft was currently being designed and built. Reliable communication over distance, both between an airplane and the ground and from one ground location to another, did not really exist yet either. But it, too, would be developed in the not too distant future. The expansion of aviation depended on it. And of course, because airplanes needed to land and take off from somewhere, more landing strips were going to be necessary in the outback.

As they pondered the maps John brought to the meeting, Hudson said he was impressed by their quality and detail. They were better than any maps Qantas was currently using. John smiled and explained that he'd found many of the maps of inland Australia quite inaccurate. If pilots were to fly safely over the outback, they were going to need accurate and detailed maps. Drawing on the vast amount of data he'd collected over the years, John had set to work with Norman Orr, a retired draftsman who volunteered his time, to draw new and accurate maps of inland Australia.

"I must compliment you," Hudson told John, "on your enterprise on such a fine production, particularly because it gives our backcountry the prominence it so urgently deserves."

John offered to provide Hudson and Qantas with a number of copies of the maps. By the time the meeting was over, John and Hudson had become firm friends. They agreed to meet together regularly, and Hudson promised to do whatever he could to make John's vision of an aerial medical service a reality.

In December 1921, two weeks after his meeting with Hudson Fysh, John received more encouraging news. This time it was in the form of a letter from the prime minister of Australia, William Hughes. John tore open the official envelope and began to read.

Dear Mr. Flynn,

. . . Commissioners who . . . returned from a visit to the Northern Territory have brought before me the necessity for providing nursing facilities for the hardy pioneers who are laboring under innumerable difficulties developing the outlying portions of our great continent.

The Government recognizes the excellent work your Mission is doing, and is not only desirous, but anxious to help as far as its resources permit. . . . The Government is prepared to contribute on the basis of £2 for every £1 raised by the citizens up to £2,000. Further the Government will endeavor—though it cannot promise—to make an aeroplane available in the district, and in addition will make enquiries with a view to ascertaining whether it is possible to install a system of wireless telephony.

I trust the assistance thus rendered will enable you to in some measure overcome the difficulties and relieve the hardships with which these progressive Australian citizens are faced.

Yours sincerely,
W. M. Hughes,
Prime Minister.

This was the best Christmas present John could ever have asked for. The prime minister of Australia was behind the work of the Australian Inland Mission, and the two thousand pounds the government was offering would go a long way toward new nursing homes and the staff necessary to run them.

In expanding the number of nursing homes in the outback, John would normally wait until some dramatic event occurred in an area that demonstrated to the locals the need for a medical treatment facility. This way, when the locals got together and decided to approach AIM to establish a nursing home in their community, they were willing to support it with their money, their time, and sometimes their facilities. This approach had worked well in Hall's Creek and Maranboy, where the nursing homes were flourishing and enjoying solid local support. John wondered if that might be the problem in Alice Springs. It had been his vision for AIM from the beginning to have a nursing home there. The locals had thought that the nursing home was a good idea, but when work began on the facility, they hadn't supported it with their money or their time as the residents of Hall's Creek and Maranboy had.

John did not have to wait too long to find out where the next nursing home should be established. In October 1922 an urgent telegraph arrived in

Darwin stating that a malaria outbreak had occurred at Victoria River Downs in the north of the Northern Territory. Eleven percent of the population had died from the disease, and urgent medical help was needed. At that time, two AIM nurses had recently arrived in Darwin and were on their way to Maranboy to replace the nurses there. A message dispatched to the two nurses was intercepted at Katherine on their train journey south. The nurses left the train and traveled westward two hundred miles to Victoria River Downs, where they took charge of the malaria outbreak. They set up a hospital in a large homestead on the banks of the Wickham River and set to work treating the sick. Soon the outbreak was contained, and the two nurses traveled on to Maranboy.

After receiving a report of the incident from the nurses, John was not surprised when the local residents at Victoria River Downs wrote to him asking for AIM to establish a nursing home in their community. They had already collected 540 pounds for it. John immediately approached the Northern Territory government, which pledged 1,080 pounds toward the project. Construction of a building to house the nursing home was soon under way. The Victoria River Downs nursing home opened in 1923.

As John worked to raise money for the expansion of AIM and coordinated the supplies and staff needed to keep the nursing homes functioning, his thoughts were never far from starting an aerial medical service. However, his plans for such a service were clouded with frustration. John kept in regular contact with Hudson, who informed him that there was still no airplane large enough to carry a patient on a stretcher. And little progress had been made toward developing landing strips in the outback. But more frustrating was the lack of a cheap radio system that could be used to call for a doctor. Of course, there was also the lack of funds for such a service. The AIM board continually reminded John that only 137 pounds had been set aside in an account for his grand aerial scheme.

John knew that the board members would be happy if he abandoned his airplane idea altogether and just concentrated on nursing homes, nurses, and patrol padres, but he couldn't do that. No matter how long it took or how difficult it proved to be, John was convinced that an aerial medical service was needed to save lives in inland Australia. He also believed that before too long, AIM airplanes would be flying sick patients out of the outback to hospitals for lifesaving care.

During 1923 John received a letter from the residents of Birdsville in southwestern Queensland requesting that AIM establish a nursing home in their community. The letter told how a woman in the community had given birth to healthy twins. However, because of the inexperience of the new mother and a lack of medical help, both twins died three weeks after birth. John was aware that Birdsville, located 1,185 miles west of Brisbane and just seven miles north of the state's border with South Australia, was one of the most isolated communities in the

Australian outback. The small community serviced a number of large cattle and sheep stations in the area. It was a hot and dry place and received supplies only twice a year. These supplies were brought in on the backs of camels from Marree in South Australia, 280 miles to the south, via the Birdsville Track. John had ridden over the same trail to Birdsville with tracker Lou Reese twelve years before when he was the Smith of Dunesk missionary. He knew just how cut off the community was from the outside world.

Not wanting to wait until money was raised and a new building erected before the nursing home was opened, John swung into action. He arranged for AIM to rent a small, abandoned hotel in the settlement for the nursing home and recruited two nurses to run it. Grace Francis and Catherine Boyd were soon on their way to Birdsville.

Not too long afterward John received a letter from tracker Lou Reese, who'd escorted the two nurses on the last leg of their journey to Birdsville. Lou explained that on the journey they came upon a four-year-old boy sick with typhoid fever. The two nurses had stopped on the track for several days to treat the boy. Lou was deeply impressed by their dedication, compassion, and calmness as they treated the child, who would otherwise surely have died. "If ever angels come on earth, I'd say these were two," Lou wrote of Grace and Catherine in his letter. John smiled: these two nurses were the embodiment of Christian charity and all that AIM stood for.

In a report from the nurses in Birdsville, John learned that conditions were more primitive than they'd expected and that the state of health was poor among the residents, particularly the children. The nurses were also still waiting for their luggage and medical equipment to arrive by camel train. In the meantime, they were using old boxes as tables and chairs in the nursing home and had borrowed kitchen utensils from the community to cook and eat their meals. Until the dentist chair arrived, the children coming for dental care were forced to sit on an old box. But Grace and Catherine were happy and content and felt that even without all their equipment, they were having an impact in the town and surrounding area.

Early in 1924, John decided to make the long trek to Birdsville to check on the nursing home's progress. He was pleased by what he found. Grace and Catherine's luggage and equipment had arrived on Christmas Eve, and the nursing home and the women's living quarters were now fully equipped. Members of the local community told John how much they appreciated the two nurses and spoke of the impact they'd already had on the place. One man told John how he virtually had to drag his injured mate to see the nurses because he didn't want women fussing over him. The injured man had ended up staying in the nursing home a week until he was completely recovered. "Now he says he'd ride five hundred miles for those two nurses to look at his next injury!" the friend said with a chuckle.

During the visit, Nurse Grace confided in John, "It's a bit scary, you know."

"Why's that?" John asked.

"They all think we can fix everything. We're only nurses, though, not doctors."

John thought for a moment and then with a twinkle in his eye said, "One day a doctor will be flying out of these skies when you most need him. I promise."

Later in 1924, John received the letter he'd been waiting for. Hudson Fysh had found the right plane for an aerial medical service, a DH 50A, made in England by the de Havilland Aircraft Company. The plane had an enclosed passenger cabin and a wide lifting door at the top through which a stretcher could fit. Hudson wrote that Qantas had already ordered a DH 50A from England and was working on a plan to be able to manufacture the de Havilland airplane in Australia under license. That way there would be enough of the planes available to cover the inland.

John could hardly wait to pass along this news to the AIM board members. Surely now they would be excited about the possibilities of using airplanes in the outback. But they were not. They raised the same old problems and objections, especially the lack of funds and there being no easy way for those living in the inland to contact such a service. No one on the board could see how such problems as these would resolve themselves in the next ten years.

Once again John could barely believe the lack of vision on the part of the board members. He was tempted to argue with them, but he knew it was pointless. Instead, he decided they all needed some time apart. John was having difficulty getting anyone to pick up and finish the building of the new nursing home at Alice Springs. *Surely there was no better place to lie low for a while than in the outback,* John reasoned. And there was one more thing. Since no one had yet invented a wireless radio that was cheap and durable enough to serve the inland, John decided to do it himself. He set himself the goal of having a machine to test within six months' time. Then he would take the device with him to Alice Springs.

Chapter 10

Hopelessly Bogged Down

"Y̶ou aren't serious, are you?" David Wyles asked. David, a radio expert in Sydney, was an elder in the Presbyterian Church.

"Very serious," John replied. "I want to know what you think the biggest obstacles will be."

David shook his head. "You may have to face the fact that it can't be done, but since you asked, here are the challenges you need to overcome." He took a deep breath and poured himself another cup of tea. "First, the cost. You're talking about each radio set costing hundreds of pounds. And don't forget you'll have to set up mother stations for the operators to be in contact with. Those will cost thousands." David stopped for a moment to stir his tea. "But assuming money was not a problem, the sets need electricity to run. Not many homes in the outback have electricity, do they?"

"No," John replied.

"Well then, you'd have to supply them with batteries—more expense, especially since extreme heat is hard on batteries. They wouldn't last long or be that reliable."

John nodded. "Another challenge. Anything else?"

"To be honest, the biggest problem is probably going to be Morse code. It takes time and determination to become good at it. I wonder how many bush people will be willing to put in the effort ahead of an emergency."

"What about telephony?" John asked. "I've read how some amateur radio enthusiasts have transmitted their voices with their equipment. Could the outbackers do that?"

"It's not possible over the distances you're thinking about. The power supply isn't strong enough. You might be able to get a voice to transmit from one side of Sydney to the other, but not one side of the country to the other. We're not there yet. Probably won't be for ten or twenty years."

"I can't wait that long," John said. "Something has to be done. Do you know someone who could help me?"

David paused for a moment. "If you're sure you want to do this, I know the best person out there. Let me ask him if he's interested."

A week later, John received a letter from George Towns. George had been a wireless operator during the war. David had spoken to him, and George was willing to work with John for six months free of charge in his quest for a workable radio in the outback. John was ecstatic.

In preparation for traveling to Alice Springs, John had ordered a Dodge buckboard. Two patrol padres now used cars to travel their circuits, and John had been impressed by how much faster and easier it made their travel in the outback. But John wanted a vehicle in which he could carry more cargo than fitted into a car. Hence the buckboard, which was made by cutting the back off a four-door Dodge car and putting a truck bed on the back instead. The Dodge John bought was being converted to a buckboard by a company in Adelaide. John intended to take delivery of it there ahead of his trip inland to Alice Springs. He arranged for George to meet him in Adelaide.

At the beginning of May 1925, John met George and immediately liked him. George was forty years old, just five years younger than John, and over six feet tall. An experienced miner and prospector, he understood the hardships of the inland and what lay ahead for the two men.

In Adelaide, John and George visited Harry Kauper, with whom John had been corresponding. Harry was chief engineer at the recently established Australian Broadcasting Commission. He had up-to-date knowledge on most aspects of radio in Australia. Harry also had a large workshop equipped with the latest radio and testing equipment and invited

John and George to make use of it while they were in Adelaide.

Soon John and George were busy building voice and Morse code radio transmitters and receivers, which they planned to test in the inland. As they worked, they encountered many problems, which, with Harry's help, they were able to overcome. They also constructed a forty-foot-tall antenna from four lengths of metal pipe. The pipes could be bolted together in the field and the antenna erected into place using a block and tackle. They also acquired large batteries to power the equipment and a generator to charge the batteries.

As the equipment began to pile up, John wondered how it would all fit on the Dodge buckboard. He'd had four extra leaves added to the vehicle's back springs to stiffen the suspension, since batteries and radio equipment were heavy. Nonetheless, he was concerned about just how much weight the Dodge could bear.

Looking at the pile, John asked, "If we're taking a generator, why not use it as our power source and leave the batteries behind?"

"Radios require steady voltage," George replied, "and the generator doesn't have a steady enough output."

"Couldn't we jack up the Dodge and connect a generator via a drive belt to the hub? That way we could run the vehicle at a constant speed. Wouldn't that generate a constant voltage?" John asked as he studied the car.

George thought a minute and then said, "Let's give it a try."

John backed the Dodge into the workshop. They added an adapter wheel to the outside of the left-hand back hub, around which a belt would run. With the hub adapter in place, they mounted a generator on the splashboard, the metal plate that replaced the Dodge's back fenders, placed a jack beneath the rear axle, and jacked up the vehicle. Once the belt from the hub adapter was attached to the generator, John climbed in and started the Dodge. After some trial and error to keep the belt straight and in place, they discovered that fourteen miles an hour seemed to be the optimal speed to produce the smoothest output of current.

"It's promising," George said when they finished the test, "but it's still not steady enough." He thought for a minute. "We should try a different generator with better windings. That could give us a smoother output."

John ordered another generator from Sydney. As soon as it arrived, he and George ripped it from its wooden crate and mounted it on the Dodge. Once again they repeated their experiment. The constant output was better this time but still not good enough for their purposes. John ordered yet another generator from Sydney with even better windings, but it, too, came up short. John could scarcely believe it. How hard was it to get a constant voltage to run radio equipment?

"Wait a minute," Harry said. "Why didn't I think of this sooner? I remember a young electrician by the name of Alf Traeger. He had me test a six-hundred-volt high-tension generator a while back. It was very good. I wonder if he still has it. That might solve your problem."

"Where can I find him?" John asked.

"At Hannan Brothers, that's where he works."

John took off running. When he reached the Hannan Brothers workshop, he made his way over to a young man winding an armature for a car generator. "Are you Alf Traeger?" he asked.

"Yes, sir," the young man said.

"Do you still have that six-hundred-volt generator you had Harry Kauper test?"

"I do," Alf said.

"I need to buy it. How much is it?"

Alf scratched his head. "What's it for?"

"The outback," John replied. "I'm working to bring radio to the outback, and I need a better generator than the ones I've been able to find. Harry says yours is the best he's seen."

"Wireless in the outback?" Alf said, raising his eyebrows. "That sounds ambitious."

For once John didn't want to chat about his project. He just wanted the generator. "How much?" he asked again.

"Twenty-nine pounds and ten shillings."

"Done," John said, fishing in his pocket for his wallet. He would have gladly paid twice that price if the generator solved his problem.

Much to John's relief, Alf's generator did the job, outputting a constant enough voltage to run the radio equipment.

Meanwhile, twenty-six-year-old Dr. George Simpson joined John and George Towns in Adelaide. He had been a ten-year-old boy in Sunday school at Andrew Barber's church in Hamilton, Victoria, when he first heard John speak while on his mission to shearers. He had followed John and his mission work ever since. George was on his way to London for postgraduate study in obstetrics. To get to England cheaply, he'd signed on as a ship's surgeon and was waiting for his vessel to dock in Adelaide. George offered to help John and George Towns prepare for their trip inland. Besides being a medical doctor, George Simpson was an expert motor mechanic. Since there were no garages, few cars, and even fewer auto mechanics in the outback, he suggested it would be good for John to know exactly how the Dodge worked and what to do when it broke down.

John agreed. Much to his surprise, George began stripping the new buckboard down until it wasn't much more than a pile of parts. Then painstakingly he began putting it back together. John took lots of notes and drew diagrams as George explained each step to him. By the time they were finished and the buckboard was once again back together, John had a thorough understanding of the vehicle. George also scrutinized the spare parts the men would carry with them on the journey in case of a breakdown, making sure the parts were securely packed.

The final preparation step was to apply to the postmaster general's office for a private radio license. AIM was given the call sign 8AC. From now on John would begin and end his radio transmissions with that code. As he loaded up the Dodge, he prayed that their efforts would pay off and 8AC would be heard all over the inland. Even with the extra leaves in the springs, the buckboard sagged under the weight of all their equipment, spare parts, luggage, food, cooking and camping gear, and enough gasoline and oil for the journey. Now it was time to head north into the inland to see if it would all work.

John and George left Adelaide at the end of June after nearly two months of preparation. Their first stop was Beltana, 350 miles to the north. John had devised a zigzag route from Adelaide that would take them through Beltana, Innamincka, Birdsville, Marree, and Oodnadatta before they reached Alice Springs. All along the way they would test their radio equipment.

In Beltana, John and George erected the antenna atop the nearest hill and set up their radio equipment. Because radio waves carry farther at night, they waited until dark to begin their first radio test. Harry in Adelaide and two amateur radio enthusiasts in Sydney had agreed to listen for their signal and respond to it.

"This is 8AC calling 5CL. Do you read me 5CL?" George said into the radio microphone, hoping to rouse Harry.

John and George listened for a response. All they heard was crackle and static. George repeated the call several times, but there was still no reply from Harry. He switched to sending Morse code over the radio, but that didn't produced a response either. During the next day, they took their radio equipment apart to check it and then put it back together. A fault was found and repaired, but it made no difference. Night after night as they broadcast, John and George received no reply to their signal.

After a week at Beltana they moved on. As they crisscrossed the desert, each night they would erect the antenna on a high spot, set up their radio gear, jack up the rear of the Dodge buckboard and run the generator to power their equipment as they broadcast using both voice and Morse code. Night after night they experienced nothing but frustration, as the only thing they heard in response was static.

One night they heard the sound of dots and dashes responding to their transmission. The message was coming from Adelaide. Their signal was reaching that far. George sent Morse code messages to Melbourne and Sydney and received responses from radio amateurs in each city. Their radio signal was reaching from the inland to the coast of Australia. John was jubilant. They were on their way, but much more work had to be done to make radio usable in the outback.

John and George pulled into Oodnadatta nine weeks after setting out from Adelaide. The nurses from the AIM nursing home rushed to meet them. As John dusted himself off from the day's drive, one of the nurses told him that their voice broadcasts had been heard. Apparently, a science student from Adelaide University had been at Murnpeowie Station, 250 miles away, where he'd been conducting some experiments. The student had a small, two-valve radio receiver with him, and when he passed through Oodnadatta on his way back to Adelaide, he reported to the nurses that he'd heard John's and George's voices over the radio, and not just once but several times over successive nights. John was amazed. He thought that their voice experiments had been a failure. But someone had heard them several hundred miles across the desert. "Perhaps voice transmission is possible out here after all, without the locals having to learn Morse code," he said to George. He hoped that would be the case because it would make things so much easier.

Now it was time to head north to Alice Springs. As the Dodge crested a rise, the settlement was spread before them. John could see the foundation of the abandoned AIM nursing home site on Todd Street in the middle of town. Driving into Alice Springs was a low point in John's life. The nursing home and the radio, which was needed to make an aerial medical service feasible, were his dreams. He believed passionately that God wanted him to bring them into being, but both were hopelessly bogged down. During the fifteen-hundred-mile zigzag journey from Adelaide, John and George had come to realize that their greatest challenge regarding radio in the outback was finding a way to power the radio without having to use a car to generate electricity. Sheep and cattle herders, camel men, and miners did not have cars, and probably never would.

In Alice Springs the pair settled into a small iron shed and sought a way to generate electricity without using the Dodge. They did not succeed, and John's spirits sank even lower when George, with nothing more to do, decided it was time for him to return to Sydney.

With little hope of making a breakthrough on his own with the radio, John turned to the other failed project—the nursing home. Although money had been set aside for the completion of the nursing home, funding was not the worst of John's problems. Getting qualified workmen, equipment, and supplies to Alice Springs were his daunting challenges.

Before leaving Adelaide, John had hired two carpenters and a cook to come to Alice Springs to work with him on the project. Soon he was headed south in the Dodge buckboard to the railhead at Oodnadatta to pick up the carpenters and cook. Once the carpenters and cook were settled at Alice Springs, work on the nursing home resumed. John labored hard beside the men, doing whatever needed to be done. It was backbreaking work, and John's already lean body grew leaner. But John pushed himself on.

Getting building supplies was a constant challenge. Many of the supplies were brought in on the backs of camels, but this was a slow process that often left the workers waiting for things to arrive. To speed up the supply process, John spent a lot of time driving hundreds of miles back and forth across the outback between Oodnadatta and Alice Springs transporting supplies that had been sent by train from Adelaide. On these trips, when he needed to make repairs to the Dodge, he was thankful for the detailed instructions George Simpson had given him. But more than breakdowns, sand was his enemy. The windblown sand was constantly moving, often piling across the track, causing the Dodge buckboard to become stuck. As he inched his way across the deep rivers of sand, John had to dig the sand away from the front of the wheels with a shovel and place boards or strips of fiber matting to keep the wheels from sinking deeper. Despite it all, John kept going. He was determined that the nursing home would be completed this time.

As John labored away in Alice Springs, his personal secretary, Thomas Ramage, would keep him up to date on the various facets of mission business by letter and telegraph from the AIM office in Sydney. One of these communications in late October 1925 brought sad news. Patrol padre Frank Brady, who worked the circuit out of Broome, Western Australia, died from malaria while undertaking a seventeen-hundred-mile circuit. In the meantime, his wife was carrying on in Broome, but a new padre would have to be found as soon as possible. John was deeply saddened by Frank's death. Frank had been a dedicated padre and was much loved and respected by the local people. John also wondered if the outcome might have been different had there been an aerial medical service to carry Frank from the field to a hospital for urgent medical care.

The following month, John received more sad news. This time it was about Thomas, who had died suddenly in Sydney. Thomas had been a tireless worker who took much of the administrative load off John's shoulders at the Sydney office. John would miss him. He also was concerned about who might be able to take care of all the office tasks, since he could not yet leave Alice Springs and return to Sydney. That person turned out to be Jean Baird, whom the AIM board named as Thomas's replacement. John was relieved. He knew Jean, who had been a part of his office team since 1922. She was a competent woman who was well versed in the inner workings of AIM.

June 26, 1926, was marked as the grand opening day for the new Alice Springs nursing home. John was exhausted as he prepared for a large group of AIM workers and supporters, including politicians, who were coming to celebrate. They would need food and lodging, and since there weren't enough accommodations for them all in the town, many would have to sleep in tents on the front lawn of the police station.

A month before the opening ceremony, John made one more trip to Oodnadatta, this time to pick up Ellen Small and Ina Pope, the two nurses who would run the nursing home. When they reached Horseshoe Bend on the way back to Alice Springs, they encountered a seriously ill man. The two nurses examined the man and determined that the patient would need to be taken to Oodnadatta. John turned the Dodge around and, with the sick man stretched out on the back of the buckboard, headed south again. By the time John and the nurses made it to Alice Springs, they were exhausted. The trip had been harrowing.

On the way back it had rained, turning the ground to mud and bogging down the Dodge. As they made their way north, they all had to stop and clamber around in knee-deep mud keeping planks and fiber mats under the wheels. The nurses were dirty and tired, but John was impressed with the way they had kept their spirits up throughout the whole ordeal. It had been quite an introduction for them to the hardships of life in the outback.

As the guests began to arrive in Alice Springs for the official opening, John knew that he looked thin and gaunt. He also knew that once the ceremony was over and the finishing touches were completed on the nursing home, his work at Alice Springs would be finished. He was not eager to leave, however. He knew that when he left Alice Springs, he would have to return to Sydney and face the members of the AIM board who were going to pressure him to give up his plan for an aerial medical service once and for all or lose his position as superintendent of the mission. John dreaded the whole ordeal, though he was thankful for the astute letters he'd been receiving from Jean Baird apprising him of the mood of the board and what to expect upon his return.

Still, when the three cars and two trucks carrying the guests made it to Alice Springs, John put on his happy face as he greeted them. Among the guests were his sister, Rosetta; the Right Reverend James Crookston, moderator general of the Presbyterian Church in Australia; and Robert Mitchell. Robert had been the first Smith of Dunesk missionary and was present at the opening of the nursing home in Ood-nadatta fifteen years before. The mission work of the Presbyterian Church in inland Australia had grown so much since that time. John knew, however, that this was not the time to rest on their laurels. They still had much missionary work to do in the countryside.

John was particularly delighted when his old friend Andrew Barber showed up for the opening. After their greeting, Andrew took John aside and with a somber look said, "I have bad news for you. Hugh Victor McKay is dead."

John's heart stopped. He had always counted on Hugh McKay to encourage him on. Also, Hugh had promised that when the time was right, he would donate money to get an aerial medical service off the ground. Now even that hope was gone.

"But all might not be lost," Andrew went on. "I don't know any of the details, but I believe that just before he died, Hugh gave instructions for some money to be left to AIM for you to use."

Now John was eager to leave Alice Springs and learn more about the money Hugh McKay had left to AIM.

Chapter 11

The Silence Is Broken

Upon his return from Alice Springs, John hurried to see Hugh McKay's lawyer in Melbourne. He learned that Hugh had handed him two amazing gifts: the first was two thousand pounds to start an experimental aerial service, with the promise of that amount each year if it proved successful; the second was the tremendous boost of being able to say that the leading industrialist in Australia had believed in and supported John's dream of a medical aerial service to provide a mantle of safety in the outback.

John smiled as he told Andrew the news. "And not only that," he continued, "my secretary Jean Baird tells me that several of the older AIM board members who have constantly opposed the idea of airplanes are going to resign. I believe that God has given us a fresh opportunity!"

And so it seemed. Back in Sydney, on September 9, 1926, the AIM board gave John permission to conduct experiments in aviation, as long as he raised another five thousand pounds to supplement Hugh's bequest. John was not too worried about having to raise the money. He was certain that people would donate toward it knowing that Hugh had backed the plan with a bequest. What did concern John was the radio problem. Unless that was solved, there would be little point in having airplanes flying over the outback.

John paid Harry Kauper another visit to seek more advice. Harry told him it was still impossible to imagine two-way radio conversations in remote areas. "The expense of the transmitter would be far too high. Not only that—it would be dangerous since it's so bulky."

"I don't have much time," John told him. "What would you advise me to do?"

Harry shook his head. "I know we've talked about it before, and I know you don't like the idea, but the only way I can see to have two-way communication would be to place one powerful mother station in a central location that could use voice radio transmissions. Then have smaller, more portable stations in the outlying areas that use Morse code to communicate. That way in an emergency a local operator could Morse code a message from the daughter station to the mother station, and the mother station operator could talk back over the radio to make sure the Morse code message was correct and to ask additional questions."

"Which would have to be answered in Morse code as well," John added.

"Exactly."

"The biggest problem is the outbacker," Harry continued. "Many of them can't spell—some of them can hardly read. I remember a story the storekeeper at Blood's Creek told me. An old prospector out there wrote out his grocery order and sent it in once a month with someone who was passing by. One time he ordered twelve bars of soap, which confused the storekeeper because a man in the bush is being overly clean if he washes once a month. Still, the storekeeper sent the soap. The prospector showed up soon after and asked the storekeeper why he had sent him soap. 'But that's what you asked for,' he said. 'Did not!' the prospector retorted. 'I asked for twelve onions, and I get bloomin' soap. What would I want with soap? I got the name right off the box of onions you sent last time. Copied it proper, I did.'" Harry smiled and then continued. "As you can see, the old prospector had no idea what the difference between the word *soap* and the word *onion* was. It's hard to imagine that we could expect someone like that to spell out words in Morse code."

"I know it's not ideal," Harry said, "but I don't see anything else that would be a better solution. Come back in twenty years and there is sure to be one."

John sat in silence. He hated to admit it, but Harry

was right. "Well then, that's what we'll start with," he said. "Anything is better than nothing at this stage. Hugh's bequest has created a lot of interest in the aerial medical service, and I'm afraid if we wait any longer, the public's enthusiasm, not to mention that of the AIM board, will dwindle."

John and Harry then discussed the various pieces of equipment that would be needed to set up such a system and which batteries would be the best to power the daughter stations. They also talked about the equipment and power requirements for the mother station. Eventually Harry provided John with some equipment he and another man had built that John could take along and test for its suitability in the daughter stations. John was encouraged when AWA Ltd., a manufacturer of radio equipment in Sydney, donated the expensive fifty-watt equipment needed to outfit a mother station. The AIM board agreed that John could go to Alice Springs in October to test the equipment and the mother-and-daughter station concept.

Now all John needed was a good electrician and radioman to go with him. He'd wanted to take George Towns along once more, but George was having health problems and was unable to go. Once again John turned to Harry for help. He asked him if he knew anyone who might be willing to join him in the outback to work with radios.

"Why not Alf Traeger?" Harry suggested.

"Oh, yes, the young man who made the six-hundred-volt generator. I remember him. I didn't get much of a chance to talk to him, though. What's he been up to lately?"

"Oddly enough, he just got his ham radio license, and he's been experimenting with radio in the shed at the back of his house. He's a devout Lutheran. I think he might just be the man you're looking for," Harry said enthusiastically.

John contacted Alf and invited him to dinner. Over roast lamb the two men talked about John's vision for the outback and how it depended upon radio. "Is that something you'd be interested in?" John asked.

Alf nodded. "I'm ready for a challenge. I've been a bit bored lately, and I've always wanted to see the outback. Now is as good a time as any, and I will be helping people as well," he said.

John nearly jumped out of his chair as he reached across the table to shake Alf's hand. "Done!" he exclaimed. "We have a lot to do. Let's start with making a list of the equipment you think we'll need to take with us."

The two men planned into the night.

In early October 1926, John and Alf, accompanied by crates of equipment, caught the train north to Oodnadatta. They picked up the Dodge buckboard, which John had left there, loaded it with equipment, and headed for Alice Springs. Among the equipment they carried was a surprise for the nurses at the new nursing home.

The two men arrived safely in Alice Springs, mostly without incident except for being bogged down several times in rivers of sand that had John and Alf crawling around, sliding boards beneath the wheels. At Alice Springs they were warmly greeted at the AIM nursing home by nurses Ellen Small and Ina Pope. Before unloading the Dodge, John and Alf sat down with the two nurses on the veranda for a cup of tea and some fresh homemade scones.

"You remember Bill Hayes?" Ellen asked John as they talked over their tea and scones.

"Indeed," John said. "How could I forget?"

Bill had been one of two local men who opposed the building of the Alice Springs nursing home, calling it too extravagant for the region. He had written numerous letters to various newspapers around the Northern Territory, attacking John and the work of AIM in Alice Springs. His actions had annoyed John at the time, but John was too exhausted from all the work getting the nursing home finished to respond. In truth, John rarely rebutted criticism of him from others. He liked to let his actions speak of his character and Christian faith.

"Bill ended up being our first patient," Ellen said with a twinkle in her eye. "The Lord works in mysterious ways."

John nodded. "Yes, He does. How did that happen?"

"Bill was brought in to us by some of his mates. He'd fractured his femur when his horse threw him. He was fifty miles away at the time. It was a very bad break, and we needed a traction machine, which we didn't have. We telegraphed a doctor in Darwin who sent back instructions for building one. We had to find various bits and pieces but managed to make one and place Bill's leg in it."

"It was an unwieldy contraption, but it worked," Nurse Ina added.

"How ironic," John said.

"Yes, but there's more. We had to keep him in traction for seventy-six days, and during that time we did everything we could to make him happy. Every day we could see him warming up to us little by little, until by the time he was discharged, we were best of friends. He made a large donation to the nursing home and now tells everyone how necessary it is and how grateful he is to us for being here."

"Wonderful news," John said. "I like to think that the best way to get rid of an enemy is to make him into a friend. And how do you find the ventilation system?"

"It works beautifully. In fact, we have many visitors who just happen to want a tour of the hospital on some of the hottest days."

"Or a second or third tour," interjected Ina.

John chuckled. "That's wonderful to hear. I have a surprise for you. Alf here is going to help with another innovation. He's an electrician, and we have the equipment to wire up the nursing home with electric lights."

The two nurses were delighted. "How wonderful! The kerosene lamps are so smelly. I can't wait until we can merely flick a switch and get light," Ellen said.

After they had finished their tea, John and Alf unloaded the Dodge buckboard and set up their work area. Their first task was to install an electric generator powered by a five-horsepower Lister diesel engine in the separate shed that had been built for that purpose behind the nursing home. Once the generator was installed, Alf ran electric wires throughout the nursing home and installed electric lights. Ellen and Ina were gleeful the first night the generator burst into life and the electric lights were flicked on.

On the opposite side of the generator shed, John and Alf installed their mother station radio equipment, which the generator also powered. Using the antenna that was still in place from a year before when John and George Towns had been experimenting, they made contact with Harry in Adelaide utilizing voice telephony. Their radio signal from Alice Springs was loud and clear.

Once the mother station in Alice Springs was up and running, John and Alf loaded up the Dodge buckboard in the early hours of November 11, 1926. They were hoping to make it to the Hermannsburg mission station, eighty miles to the west, before it got dark. Hermannsburg was a Lutheran mission working among the Aborigines. As they drove west over a deeply rutted track, John told Alf the story of Carl Strehlow, the mission founder.

"He was a brilliant man, you know, especially with languages," John began. "He picked up the Aranda language in just two years and started translating the New Testament into it. But the isolation got him. In 1922 he got sick with dropsy, and his wife knew he needed medical help. They loaded him into a cart and started out for the Oodnadatta railway station, but they only made it 150 miles. Carl died at Horseshoe Bend, where they buried him. If we'd had an aerial medical service at the time, his life could well have been saved."

"And that was just four years ago? Sounds like something that should have happened a hundred years ago."

"You're right there," John agreed. "That's life in the outback. But with airplanes and radio we're going to transform the inland, if we can just figure out how to make it all work."

The bumpy, dusty journey came to an end as the Dodge pulled to a halt in front of the Hermannsburg mission station. The sun was beginning to set.

That night John and Alf sat down with Pastor Albrecht, who ran the mission, and Adolph Heinrich, the mission teacher. Both men were fascinated with the possibility of radio and airplanes in the outback. "Months go by without our seeing anyone except the Aborigines. The nearest European settlers out here in the bush are miles away. Your radio and your airplanes will help connect us," Pastor Albrecht commented. "The Aborigines will be served too if they accept your flying doctor help, though they have their own medicines and witch doctors and are suspicious of the ways of the settlers."

The following morning, a large group of Aborigines watched as John and Alf erected a thirty-foot radio aerial on a rise near the mission house. John and Alf then set up their radio equipment in the house, connected it to the batteries, and gave Pastor Albrecht and Adolph a basic education in Morse code.

After the sun had gone down, it was time to make contact with the mother station in Alice Springs, where Maurie Fuss, the local telegraph operator, had been left to man the radio. Alf placed headphones over his ears and began to tap out a message in Morse code. "8AD calling 8AB. Come in 8AB. Over." He waited expectantly for the voice of Maurie over the radio, but there was only static. He repeated the message numerous times, but nothing.

Early the next morning Alf took the radio apart, searching for a fault in it, but he could find none. As far as he could tell, the radio was working perfectly. He tried once more to contact Maurie at 8AB, the mother station in Alice Springs. Still no reply. He tapped out another Morse code message and this time received return messages from several radio hams who heard the message. Harry Kauper in Adelaide signaled that he'd heard it too. Alf knew that this could mean only one thing: the problem was with the mother station back in Alice Springs.

The next morning, before the sun rose, John and Alf headed from Hermannsburg back to Alice Springs. Before leaving they had given Pastor Albrecht instructions to send a Morse code message over the radio to Alice Springs at five o'clock that afternoon. Alf hoped to have the mother station radio problem fixed by then.

As it turned out, the journey back to Alice Springs took longer than expected, and they didn't arrive until three minutes to five. Alf didn't even wait for the car to come to a halt before jumping out and dashing to the generator shed where the radio was housed.

"Here's the problem," Alf said, pointing to a coil when John walked in. "Maurie put the wrong coil in. The radio's been tuned into the wrong frequency the whole time we were in Hermannsburg trying to make contact."

Alf looked at his watch as he placed the right coil into the radio. At exactly five o'clock the radio burst to life in a flow of dots and dashes of Morse code. They were broadcasting from Hermannsburg. Alf responded quickly by voice over the radio. "8AB calling 8AD. 8AB calling 8AD. Hear you loud and clear. Over." A jumble of Morse code began streaming over the radio from Hermannsburg. Alf tried to work out what the message said, but it was impossible, just a continual flow of dots and dashes. "Send more slowly," he broadcast to them over the radio. But still the Morse code kept bursting forth like an unstoppable machine gun. "They've forgotten all about spaces between the words. It's just a big jumble," Alf said to John.

"Looks that way," John agreed. "Perhaps they're just too excited hearing us talk to them. Let's try again in the morning. They might have calmed down by then."

Since just before sunrise was one of the best times to send and receive clear radio transmissions, John and Alf were up bright and early the next morning,

ready to see if Pastor Albrecht or Adolph had figured out how to send readable Morse code. Much to
John's delight they had. Their message came in loud
and clear, with spaces in all the right places.

With the daughter station at Hermannsburg up
and running, John and Alf set off in late November
for Arltunga, seventy miles east of Alice Springs,
where they set up a second daughter station in the
police station. Soon the two daughters were sending
Morse code messages to the mother station in Alice
Springs and receiving voice transmissions back. The
two daughter stations even began sending direct
Morse code messages to each other without going
through the mother station.

The silence of the inland had finally been broken.
Many hurdles still had to be overcome, but at least
John could report back to the AIM board that they
had successfully sent and received radio messages
across the outback.

Chapter 12

Advisors

Every answer leads to ten more questions, John thought as he stared at the notebook in front of him. All the way back from Alice Springs he'd been taking notes on the questions he'd have to find answers to when he got back to his office in Sydney: Should we buy or rent an airplane? Who should be the first flying doctor? How will we find him? How will we get the locals to prepare the landing strips? How many mother stations can we afford? Where should the first flying doctor be headquartered? What is the best way to teach people Morse code?

The questions went on page after page, and John soon came to one conclusion: he would need a large team in order to move quickly enough to get an aerial medical service up and running. This led to yet another list, this time of all the people he would like to see on his team. John listed them under three headings: Medical Advisors, Aviation Advisors, and Radio Advisors. For the plan to succeed, each group would need to involve the top people in their field. And there was one more person John sorely needed— someone to take over the daily responsibilities of AIM, freeing John to devote himself to coordinating the three groups.

One of the first things John did was call upon his old friend Andrew Barber. John did not like putting pressure on anyone, but he explained the urgency of the situation and asked Andrew if he would be willing to take time away from his own parish to help out. Andrew agreed. John was delighted. Andrew would be given the job title of Patrol Organizer. With the day-to-day running of AIM off his shoulders, John could throw his full weight into the aerial medical project.

In no time at all John had assembled the team he'd dreamed about. Two doctors, George Simpson and J. W. Dunbar Hooper of the British Medical Association of Australia, led the medical team. Lieutenant Colonel Horace C. Brinsmead, controller of Civil Aviation in Australia; Hudson Fysh from Qantas; and Lieutenant Thomas White, president of the Australian Aero Club, made up the aviation team. The radio team consisted of Alf Traeger, Harry Kauper, and Ernest T. Fisk, Managing Director of AWA, the company that had donated the radio equipment for the mother station in Alice Springs. A fourth group of general advisors consisted of Cecil and Sam McKay, representing the H. V. McKay Trust, and two members of Parliament, Michael Durack and David S. Jackson.

With his team of advisors in place, John's first task was to decide where the first flying doctor should be based. After consulting with his advisors, Cloncurry in northwestern Queensland was chosen as the base of operations. Within a radius of three hundred miles of Cloncurry, an airplane could reach into the Cape York peninsula in the north, the Northern Territory to the west, and the border with South Australia to the south. The area within this three-hundred-mile radius was studded with settlers and small settlements with populations from ten to fifty people. Cloncurry was also the site of a forty-bed government hospital with a doctor and nursing staff. Qantas maintained a well-equipped airfield there, and Cloncurry was connected to the telegraph system and had a rudimentary telephone system that reached to several nearby communities. It seemed to everyone to be the perfect location for an aerial medical service experiment.

While Cloncurry seemed to fit the bill, John wanted to be sure. Any misstep at this point could shake people's confidence in the entire project. John sent George Simpson and Andrew Barber off to Cloncurry in the Dodge buckboard to make sure the people of the town would get behind the new service. The two arrived at Cloncurry at the beginning of August 1927. According to the report John received from Andrew, the local residents were fully supportive of having an aerial medical service based in their community. This, Andrew explained, had come about because of a medical emergency that occurred the day after they arrived. A miner at Mount Isa, seventy miles west of Cloncurry, had been seriously injured in an accident and had a broken pelvis and spine. He needed urgent hospital care but was in no condition to travel overland to Cloncurry. The mining company arranged to charter a Qantas airplane to fly to Mount Isa and carry the injured man to the hospital. Dr. Simpson offered to accompany the pilot and care for the injured miner on the return flight. All had gone well, and the injured man was safely transferred to the hospital in Cloncurry, demonstrating to the town's residents how valuable doctors and airplanes could be in the outback.

The timing had been perfect. Based on Andrew's report, John wrote up an account of the Mount Isa incident and sent it off for publication in a number of influential newspapers. Then he set out to visit those groups his advisors had identified as having an active interest in helping to fund an aerial medical service. The positive publicity, along with the backing of such a distinguished group of advisors, opened many doors for John. He soon had donations of one thousand pounds from the Wool Brokers Association and the same amount from the Civil Aviation Department, and the Defense Department offered to pay half the cost of flying the airplane.

Qantas agreed to allow AIM to charter one of its new de Havilland DH50 planes, along with a top-rated pilot who knew the outback well from flying the mail run over it. John was relieved to hear this. Not just any pilot would do. The pilot would be flying by line of sight and needed an intimate knowledge of the terrain above which he was traveling. Because few airstrips existed for landing and takeoff, the pilot also needed to know where they were and how best to approach and land on them. These were details a pilot flying the mail run would know. After all, his life depended on it.

By late October, John and Alf were on their way to Cloncurry with Alf's latest experimental radio equipment loaded in the back of the Dodge buckboard. Alf had been busy, and John was eager to see how all the new equipment worked. They had a new antenna that was lighter, easier to erect, and much more efficient and a hand generator that could replace the bulky, volatile batteries that currently powered the radios. Alf explained to John how he had taken a hand-operated, bench-mounted emery wheel grinder, removed the emery wheel, and replaced it with a small generator. When the handle was turned, it spun the generator and produced a reasonable electric output. At Harry's suggestion Alf had added a quartz crystal to the circuit that smoothed out the voltage output, making it suitable for radio transmissions. Turning the device with his left hand, Alf was able to send Morse code with his right. Alf also had plans to modify the Dodge, mounting a generator on the front of the car so that it could be run directly from the car engine, instead of jacking the car up and attaching a belt to a hub extension.

Before they even reached Cloncurry, Alf had made the modification to the Dodge. The generator worked perfectly, allowing the car-powered radio to be used as a transmitting base. To John this was wonderful news. All the patrol padres now used cars. With this modification made to the cars, John could envision the padres sending and receiving radio messages on their long circuits through the outback.

John's mind, however, was soon ranging farther afield. John wondered aloud to Alf if it would be possible for a radio to be installed in an aircraft, allowing a pilot to talk to the ground. The answer was yes. In theory there was nothing to stop a pilot from talking to the ground while in flight. The only problem was that right now the equipment was too bulky. John could already imagine a time when a doctor in the air would be able to relay instructions via radio transmission to a seriously ill or injured person on the ground before he even arrived there.

When the men arrived in Cloncurry on Tuesday, November 1, 1927, John immediately realized that his timing was terrible. It was Melbourne Cup Day. The Melbourne Cup was Australia's most famous horse race. Even though the race was being run twelve hundred miles away to the south, John learned that everyone in Cloncurry had "Cup Fever," with Trivalve, one of the horses in the race, being the town's favorite to win.

John sighed. It didn't look as though he would be able to hold a meeting in town about the aerial medical service experiment until all the excitement had died down and the winner had been announced via telegraph. Suddenly inspiration struck John. "Do you think you could string up an aerial and get the Melbourne Cup tuned in on the radio?" he asked Alf.

Alf gave John a confused look. It was not the sort of question that usually came from a Presbyterian minister. And then he smiled as he realized what John was up to. "Yes, I can," he said.

Soon Alf was busy stringing an aerial in an open space behind the post office where people could gather. He set up a radio receiver, connected a battery, and began to tune in the broadcast of the race from Flemington Racecourse in Melbourne. The signal came in loud and clear. John told Alf to turn the volume up all the way.

Locals began to spill out of pubs, businesses, and homes to see where the disembodied voice they were hearing drifting across town was coming from. Soon a large crowd had gathered around the radio behind the post office, listening as an announcer spoke. "We are awaiting the start of the main race of the day, the Melbourne Cup, here at Flemington. A light rain is falling as 135,000 people wait patiently in the stands for the race to begin. And they're off . . ."

A huge cheer went up from the crowd, drowning out the race commentary. By the time they got their focus back on the radio, the race was well under way. ". . . Trivalve coming on the outside. Trivalve's taking charge with one furlong to go. One furlong to go, can she bring in the cup? Avant Courier is—"

Suddenly the radio went dead. Alf raced to find out what had gone wrong. A dog had bitten through the ground wire on the aerial. Alf worked as fast as he could to get the wire reconnected. By the time the radio burst back to life, the race was over and the announcer was reading the official placings. When he announced that Trivalve had won, another huge cheer went up as the men raised their glasses of beer in a toast. The celebrations went on well into the night.

The next evening, virtually the entire town showed up to hear John speak about the aerial medical service. Just as the emergency flight to Mount Isa during George and Andrew's visit three months before had captured the imagination of the locals, so had listening to the Melbourne Cup on the radio. John talked to the people about the aerial medical service and the wireless network that would be installed in their town. He answered their questions as best he could, though he knew there was still a lot of work to be done.

Before leaving Cloncurry for Melbourne, John helped set up a local aerial medical service committee to spread the word about the experiment, drum up more support for the service, and cooperate in planning and working out the many local details that would need to be taken care of.

On their way south from Cloncurry, John and Alf discussed the next steps they needed to take to make the experimental service a reality. The medical advisory committee needed to find the person to be the first flying doctor, and Alf needed to make the radio transmitters, and especially the receivers, hardier. Traveling the rutted tracks of inland Australia had confirmed to them that the sets were still much too fragile to be useful.

In Melbourne, John attended an AIM board meeting. The board listened attentively to his detailed progress report on setting up the experimental aerial service in Cloncurry. When he finished the report, board members congratulated him on his success thus far. However, John was not expecting what came next. The board told him it was time for him to take a year's furlough from the Australian Inland Mission.

John was dumbfounded. Yes, he'd never taken more than two or three days off at a time while working with AIM, but he explained that he considered it a holiday to visit the inland on AIM assignments. The board thought otherwise and insisted that he was tired and needed a complete break. Perhaps he should consider taking a trip around the world.

John had to admit that at the age of forty-seven he had not quite fully recovered from expending so much energy building the Alice Springs nursing home. But he couldn't leave until the Cloncurry experiment was up and running. Too much was at stake. John struck a compromise with the board. He agreed to take a furlough in a year, once the experimental aerial medical service was operating. The board agreed, and John put the matter out of his mind.

John still had much to do to get the experiment going in Cloncurry. The day before Christmas, he placed an advertisement in the *Medical Journal of*

Australia for a qualified person to become the first flying doctor. Twenty-two doctors answered the advertisement. One of them was Dr. Kenyon St. Vincent Welch. John read through his résumé with increasing interest. Dr. Welch ran a large medical practice in Sydney and was prepared to leave it and his wife and children to dedicate a year to being a flying doctor. He was a devout Christian and wanted to serve the people of the outback. After meeting with Dr. Welch in person, John liked him even more. Dr. Welch was warm and friendly and a skilled surgeon, just the kind of person who would stay positive and be useful in emergencies.

In April 1928, Dr. Welch was appointed the first flying doctor of the new Aerial Medical Service, or AMS, as it was now officially named, though it remained under the direct oversight of AIM. An experienced Qantas airman, Arthur Affleck, would become the first pilot.

John wanted the de Havilland DH50 aircraft they would be using to be called *Victor*, after Hugh Victor McKay. A sign painter was called to paint the name on the plane, but the painter mistakenly painted a *y* at the end. Thus, the airplane became *Victory*. John thought it a fitting name, though they were still far from where they needed to be. Dr. Welch and Arthur Affleck could fly to any emergency—as long as they knew about it. That confined them to cases that could be communicated by telegraph, the local telephone system, or a person coming for help for a friend or family member. It was a start, but not what John had in mind. He told Alf that the long-term success of the Aerial Medical Service now rested on him.

In the meantime, Dr. Welch started sending back just the kind of medical reports John needed. The reports were professional, detailed, and to the point, showing the potential impact of covering the entire inland with an aerial medical service. Dr. Welch and Arthur had flown to various locations to treat patients with all manner of illnesses and injuries.

Despite the good reports, Dr. Welch reported that there were some problems. He was a better qualified and more skilled surgeon than any of the doctors he encountered at the small government hospitals scattered around the region. Although he promised not to treat patients that these doctors could reach by car, some of the doctors resented his presence in the area. Worse yet, when typhoid broke out in Cloncurry, Dr. Welch offered his services, but the doctor at the local hospital refused his help. Eleven men died in the hospital as the overworked medical staff tried to treat all the cases brought to them. All Dr. Welch could do was sit by and watch the disaster unfold.

Dr. Welch wrote to John about the situation and received an encouraging reply. In his letter John outlined how he kept going when people criticized him. He wrote how he tried not to worry about short-term challenges and instead took a long view of events: "Practically all his [a man who thinks in centuries] consciousness is projected into the other side of next Christmas, and his gaze sweeps the horizon rather than the outhouse-infested foreground. As far as the

AMS is concerned, I am not at all pessimistic, and I hope you, yourself, will be incapable of that."

In October 1928, John received some sad news. His father had died. At Thomas Flynn's funeral, John thought of all the ways his father had supported him throughout his life. Although Thomas had at first resisted the idea of his son going to inland Australia as a home missionary, he had come to accept it. He developed a keen interest in outreach work in the outback and donated money to AIM whenever he could. John was grateful that his father had lived long enough to see a flying doctor in the air. John knew he would miss his father's encouragement.

Still saddened by the death of his father, a month later John received a message that cheered him up. It was from Alf. "Come and see the real 'Victory' before you go on your holiday trip." John immediately bought a train ticket to Adelaide. Because he knew that Alf was a very modest man who did not like to make a fuss, Alf would surely have something exciting to show him. And indeed he did. Sitting on a table in Alf's workshop was a compact black box covered with dials. Bolted to the floor beneath the table was a contraption with bicycle pedals sticking out on either side.

"It's a new, more compact and robust radio transceiver powered by a pedal-operated generator," Alf said quietly. "Now the operator can use his feet to generate the power for the radio instead of using one hand to spin the old hand-crank version. The principle's the same as the hand-crank generator, and it has the same quartz crystal to smooth out the power for transmissions. I've sealed the pedal unit with heavy oil inside to lubricate the gears. It should hold up to conditions in the outback. Now an operator's hands are both free to use the Morse key. It's easy enough for a woman or a child to use. What's even better, I can produce one of these pedal-powered radio transceiver sets for thirty-three pounds."

Alf sat down and gave John a demonstration of how it worked. John stood in silence watching, tears filling his eyes. "Thank you," he said at last, patting Alf on the back. Then he sat down and tried the radio himself. It worked perfectly. John knew that this was the missing piece in the radio puzzle. Now a person anywhere in the outback could generate sufficient power to operate a radio by doing nothing more than peddling evenly with his feet. John could hardly wait for Alf to begin producing more of the pedal radios.

More good news awaited John on his return to Sydney. Jean informed him that someone had sent an anonymous bank check for one thousand pounds. This was more than enough to begin manufacturing Alf's newly invented radio transceiver equipment.

As the end of his one-year term as a flying doctor with the AMS approached, Dr. Welch reported that he'd treated over two hundred patients. This included a boy with a shotgun wound to his stomach, a man who had been gored by a bull, another who'd been bitten by a deadly snake, an old man who had accidently stepped off the second-story balcony of a hotel, and a man suffering a heart attack. Dr. Welch had saved at least four lives, made fifty flights, and covered an area of twelve thousand square miles in the airplane. Given these successes, the experimental Aerial Medical Service was approved to continue for a second year. John felt a surge of relief. It was now time for him to pack his bags and take a furlough.

Chapter 13

Around the World

John climbed the gangplank and boarded the ocean liner SS *Otranto*. He was wearing his freshly cleaned wool suit. It was February 27, 1929, and it was a predictably hot summer day in Sydney. John thought it the perfect kind of day to be embarking upon a world tour. His luggage had already been taken aboard to his cabin. All he carried was his attaché case of personal papers and a copy of the *Sydney Morning Herald* tucked under his arm. Once aboard he joined the stream of passengers heading to the port railing from where they peered down at the dock.

Some of the passengers had already thrown streamers down to friends and family on the dock waiting for the vessel's departure. John searched the crowd until he found his friends, about forty of them, who had come to wave him off on his trip. He was grateful to each of them and to the many others who'd come to his farewell party the night before. They had collected six hundred pounds at the event for John to use on the trip and had presented the money to him at the end of the evening. John was flabbergasted. "We waited until the last minute to tell you," Andrew told him, "because we knew if you weren't getting on the ship tomorrow you would spend it all on wireless equipment."

John laughed as he thought about it. He knew it was true. He hardly gave any thought to money and preferred to let it pass through his hands and on to where it was truly needed. He was glad that Andrew would be taking care of mission business while he was away. Since Andrew had agreed to become a part of AIM as Patrol Organizer, he and John had formed a great partnership. John knew that AIM would be in good hands while he was gone.

As the ship's steam whistle growled loudly, signaling that departure was imminent, John felt something in his pocket. His heart dropped as he discovered the keys to the AIM office and filing cabinets. He'd been in such a hurry with his final packing he had forgotten to give them to Andrew. He cupped his hands around his mouth and yelled to Andrew, "Catch these!" He held up the keys, drew back his arm, and threw them from the ship as hard as he could. They landed near Andrew. The clip holding them together shattered on impact, scattering keys over the dock. People laughed as they picked them up and handed them to Andrew.

Jean looked up, smiled at John, and shook her head. John was pleased that she was there. If there was one person who truly understood what he was trying to achieve in his ministry, it was Jean. In the three years she had been his private secretary he'd come to trust her judgment on matters as much as he did his own. He was thankful that Jean would be the one writing weekly updates to him of what was happening at AIM. Her letters were always full of astute observations.

At noon the whistle again sounded loudly, the hawsers holding the vessel to the dock were let go, and the *Otranto* began to drift away from the dock, breaking the lines of streamers as it went. John stood at the railing and watched as the ship made its way through the Sydney harbor and out into the Tasman Sea. After unpacking his few clothes and stowing them away in his cabin, John went back up on deck. As the coast of New South Wales began to slip from view, he sat down on a deck chair to read the copy of the *Sydney Morning Herald* he'd brought with him. He knew it would be the last Australian newspaper he would read for a year.

One story in the newspaper caught his attention. It was about heavy flooding occurring in central and northern Queensland. John read:

The Commissioner of Railways announced this morning from Townsville that the Herbert

River bridge was 12 ft. 3 inches underwater.
. . . The bridge over the Seymour river was
two feet under water, which was rising. Telegraph and telephone lines on the Atherton
tableland were interrupted. Between two and
three inches of rain fell last night all along the
line between Townsville and Cairns. It would
seem that it would not be possible to get trains
through from Townsville to Cairns before the
end of the week.

Conditions sounded terrible there, but John's
mind was not focused on the conditions themselves
but on what they meant to the people living in the
affected areas. He knew that was what motivated
him. The well-being of others was always at the
forefront of his mind, and not just their physical but
also their spiritual well-being. That was what AIM
was all about—caring for people. Offering Christian
charity to address people's physical needs opened
their hearts to the "Great Father," as John liked to
refer to God. People would then listen about Chris-
tianity and consider their spiritual needs. John had
seen this happen time and time again in the outback.
That made everything that he and the AIM staff did
in the pursuit of helping people in need worthwhile
and fulfilling.

As the *Otranto* made its way through the Indian
Ocean and on into the Red Sea, John discovered that
shipboard life was rather boring. There was nothing
to see but the vast ocean and an occasional island in

the distance. What he was eager to do was to meet new people and learn from them. His intent while away was to seek out ideas for improving radio trans-missions and the use of medical rescue airplanes. To help him do this, he had brought with him the atta-ché case filled with letters of introduction to all sorts of officials around the world. He even had letters of introduction from the prime minister of Australia to the Australian High Commissioner in London, the Australian Trade Representative in Paris, and the Australian Commissioner in New York.

When the SS *Otranto* docked in Port Said, Egypt, after passing through the Suez Canal, John disem-barked. He traveled up the Nile River to Luxor and saw all sorts of ancient ruins. From Cairo, Egypt, he traveled overland through the Middle East to Con-stantinople, Turkey, and then on to London.

In London John went to Australia House to retrieve the mail awaiting his arrival. He was delighted to see several letters from Jean among the pile. He was eager to catch up on all the AIM news. At Australia House, John presented his letter of intro-duction from the prime minister. He was surprised to learn that he had been appointed as the official Aus-tralian delegate to the First International Congress on Aerial Medical Services that was to be held in Paris the following month. John was astonished to learn that there were enough countries in the world using airplanes for medical purposes to convene such a conference. He hoped to learn a lot about what oth-ers were doing and planning.

Upon his arrival at the congress in Paris, John discovered that he was one of the most sought after delegates in attendance. Everyone wanted to know how the AIM experiment with an airplane was working out and what the mission planned to work on next. Some countries, such as France, were using airplanes as military ambulances to evacuate wounded soldiers from battle. Other countries were contemplating the medical use of military planes. No other country, however, was attempting to do what was being done in Australia using civilian aircraft.

John was thankful that he had new information to pass on to the attendees. He read aloud to them a letter he'd recently received from Alf Traeger describing how he had manufactured ten of the new pedal radio transceivers. Alf and a helper, Harry Kinzbrunner, had traveled to Cloncurry, where they had set up a new two-hundred-watt radiotelephony mother station, VJ1, powered by a generator run by a Lister diesel engine. The mother station was working well, and Alf was about to go out on patrol with patrol padre George Scott to install the pedal-powered radios and new sixty-foot antennas at widely separated homesteads across the region. Alf's pedal-powered radios provoked a lot of interest at the congress in Paris.

When the First International Congress on Aerial Medical Services ended, John was invited to attend an International Conference for Inter-Church Aid in Switzerland. On his arrival in Switzerland, another letter from Alf was awaiting him. Alf reported that he had installed the first pedal radio set at Augustus

Downs cattle station, a second one at Lorraine, and a third at Gregory Downs. Patrol padre George Scott had been able to address his Sunday school class back in Cloncurry by radio from Gregory Downs. Alf and George were about to set out for Birdsville, where they planned to install the fourth pedal radio set at the AIM nursing home. As he read Alf's letter, John found it difficult to be so far away from all these new developments. He consoled himself with the knowledge that wherever he went, he was spreading the most up-to-date news on innovations in aerial medical services.

While still in Europe, John visited Germany, Belgium, and Luxemburg, before going on to Scotland, where he addressed the Assemblies of the Church of Scotland and the Free Church of Scotland. He also traveled to Ireland to do some research on his ancestry.

He then sailed across the Atlantic Ocean, arriving in New York City, home of the American Stock Exchange on Wall Street. The month before, stock prices had plummeted, causing the savings of hundreds of thousands of people to be wiped out. Already the economy in the United States was beginning to feel the effects of the stock market crash. Factories had begun cutting back their production, and many people lost their jobs as a result. John read in the newspapers about how the economic crisis was spreading to other countries as well. He was concerned about what might happen if this crisis reached Australia. It would surely make raising funds to support the ministry of AIM even harder than it had been in the past.

From New York, John traveled north to Canada, visiting Nova Scotia, Montreal, Ottawa, and Toronto. Then back in the United States he went to Washington, DC, followed by Chicago, where the temperature was below freezing. He took a train south to New Orleans and made his way westward across the deserts of the Southwest, stopping to examine several agricultural irrigation systems. From Los Angeles, California, he traveled north to San Francisco. By now John had filled notebook after notebook with plans and ideas spurred by things he had seen and experienced along the way. He had also used rolls of film to take photographs of the things he saw that might help those living in the inland of Australia.

In San Francisco it was time to board ship for the trip across the Pacific Ocean back to Australia. John arrived in Sydney on February 28, 1930, one year and one day after setting out. He felt refreshed, and although he'd turned forty-nine years old while away, he again had a spring in his step, as he had in his thirties. His attaché case was filled with facts and addresses of interesting people, and his files overflowed with newspaper clippings and pamphlets on all sorts of issues. He was eager to see his old friends again and catch up on all the news from AIM.

It didn't take long for John to notice that he had returned to a different Australia. The Wall Street stock market crash in New York had indeed triggered a worldwide financial crisis. This depression was beginning to have an effect on Australia. The nation had become wealthy exporting wool for soldiers' uniforms during the Great War. It had continued to make money exporting wool and other agricultural products to Europe as the countries there slowly recovered from the devastating effects of the fighting. But with a worldwide depression taking hold, the market for Australia's exports was quickly drying up. This was leading to the large-scale unemployment John had seen beginning in the United States.

Many things clambered for John's attention upon his return to Australia, but he was glad to see that Andrew had done a fine job overseeing the work of AIM in his absence.

At the Presbyterian Church Federal General Assembly held in September 1930, John presented a report on the Aerial Medical Service experiment in Cloncurry. To his relief and delight, the assembly agreed to continue the service "with such modification as may be necessary to meet changing circumstances." John took this to mean that the Assembly was authorizing him to go ahead and develop the AMS into a nationwide organization.

John spent his fiftieth birthday, November 25, 1930, in Sydney. He had yet to make it into the inland since his return to Australia. By now Alf was perfecting his latest invention, a typewriter-like device that turned presses of the letter keys into Morse code signals broadcast over the radio. This meant that those living in inland Australia would no longer need to learn Morse code to send radio messages. It also meant that messages could be sent much more swiftly and with better accuracy. Alf was also working on making the radio sets used in the outback even more robust and, he hoped, unbreakable.

Given the endorsement of the General Assembly, the AIM board stood behind John, agreeing that the mission should move toward implementing his grand scheme of the AMS for all of Australia. Then disaster struck. The worldwide economic depression grew worse. The Australian government told John that it would no longer be able to help pay for a flying doctor and airplane. At the same time, AIM's treasurer reported a steep drop-off in donations to the mission. Everyone in Australia was feeling the financial strain. Although John understood that, it was a crucial time for aerial medical services. The problem was, no one knew how long the depression would last or whether the AMS would survive until it ended.

Chapter 14

His "Mythical Self"

Two months later in January 1931, John sat at his office desk in Sydney wondering how the Aerial Medical Service would attract a new doctor for the coming year. Not only did the service need a new doctor, but also it needed a very special one—a doctor who could inspire the public and help keep the air service running as the economic depression squeezed more tightly. John heard Jean Baird tap on his door. "Mr. Flynn, there's someone here to see you. His name is Dr. Allen Vickers," she said.

John knew the name immediately. He hardly ever forgot a person he met. Three years before, Allen had applied to become the first flying doctor, a job that had gone to Dr. Kenyon St. Vincent Welch. John's pulse increased. Was this the man God was leading the service to? "Come in," he said. "It's so nice to see you again. Tell me, how are you doing?"

"Wonderful, Mr. Flynn. I'm on my way to Japan in a few days and then to England to take up a surgery scholarship, and I'm at a loose end. I thought I'd visit you to see how the Aerial Medical Service is coming along."

"You couldn't have come at a better time," John said, pulling out the map he'd been working on. "Take a look at this. It's our plan to expand the work at Cloncurry to cover the whole of the inland." Allen looked impressed as John pointed out the details of his plan. "We need six bases, here, here, and here."

"That means six flying doctors?" Allen said, looking puzzled.

"Yes, quite right," John replied. "That's the situation. We have only one at the moment and given the current economic conditions, even that base is in danger of closing. The government has stopped subsidizing us, and we've already had to use a thousand pounds out of the Presbyterian general fund to keep the service running. But that can't go on. The church is feeling the pinch too. If things go on as they are, I believe we'll have to suspend our operation. Trust will be broken, and the dedicated men and women who make it happen will be disbanded. It would be unlikely that the service would ever get back up and running."

"Do you have a plan?" Allen asked.

"We've had several, but they've all fallen through," John answered. "What we really need is an exceptional doctor to guide us through the crisis. I believe there's one out there. God waits until things are the blackest sometimes. Then He works in His own mysterious way, and things work out. Don't ask me how. I can't explain it, but I've seen Him work like that a number of times."

The two men talked on, John describing his vision and Allen asking questions. As they talked, John's mind whirled. Was this man sitting in front of him really the man he had been praying for? Was he the flying doctor who could get them through this crisis? As John looked into Allen's blue eyes, he had a strange conviction that he was indeed looking at that man.

"I remember you said you had an interest in radio," John continued. "We're on the verge of a breakthrough. Alf Traeger, our radioman, has made radios so small and lightweight that we're thinking of fitting one to the *Victory*. By having a radio operator on a flight, the doctor could be in touch with the patient, giving advice, checking up on the situation, even before the plane lands. It would be a first in the world. What do you think of that?"

Allen was impressed.

The two talked on. An hour passed, then another. By the time Allen left John's office, he had agreed to cancel his trip to Japan so that he could fill in as the flying doctor for three months at Cloncurry. He told John that he still expected to take up his surgery scholarship in England.

John received more good news. Kingsley Partridge returned to his old position as patrol padre on the Central Patrol. John was happy to have his friend back in AIM. Those people Kingsley had visited and ministered to were also glad to have him back, conferring on him the nickname Skipper. Before long Alf was traveling with Skipper on his patrols, installing pedal radios at the outlying communities and sheep and cattle stations as they went. AIM had four patrol padre circuits and now operated twelve nursing homes.

Meanwhile, in Cloncurry, it was not long before Allen had canceled his plans to travel to England and had signed on full-time with the AMS. John was excited. He was convinced that Allen was the man for the hour, and Allen soon proved that he was. He was a handsome and courageous young doctor who won a place in the hearts of Australians. At a time when so many people were losing their jobs, stories of Dr. Vickers and his brave antics in the outback of Queensland were just the distraction many of them needed.

One article carried in February 1932 by the newspapers under the banner headline "1,300 Mile Race with Death" particularly captured the nation's attention. The article related how in Croydon in northern Queensland a kerosene refrigerator had exploded beside a hotel keeper named Jock Williamson, inflicting a severe head injury. By the time Allen had arrived by airplane, the patient's lungs were failing. Allen decided that Jock's only hope for survival was to get him to the nearest large hospital, which was in Brisbane, thirteen hundred miles away.

Reporters picked up on the story by listening to AMS radio transmissions. They learned that Jock had been placed on a stretcher that was being carried in the *Victory*'s cramped cabin. Jock's mother sat in the only seat while Dr. Vickers sat on a petrol can tending the patient. Flying conditions were harsh. Summer temperatures soared to 122 degrees Fahrenheit, and the airplane faced strong headwinds. It made stops at Cloncurry and Winton for refueling before making it to Longreach, where the patient, his mother, and the doctor were transferred to a larger Qantas airplane and again took to the sky in a race against death. Jock died 140 miles from Brisbane. By the time the airplane made it to Archerfield landing strip in Brisbane, darkness had fallen and the landing strip was lined with flares so the pilot knew where to land. Reporters and photographers rushed forward to document the end of the thirteen-hundred-mile race with death. A hush fell over the crowd as Dr. Vickers broke the news that his patient had died.

John picked up his morning newspaper. He was amazed to see the headline, and he read the story quickly. Of course, he couldn't have asked for better publicity. Instead of viewing the death of Jock Williamson as a failure of the flying doctor, Australians were reminded of why it was so important to get medical help to those who lived in the inland. Donations to the Aerial Medical Service began to grow, and the newspapers asked Allen Vickers to write regular reports of his medical air excursions.

John was glad to see Allen getting due public recognition. He liked to stay out of the public eye, quietly encouraging people and making sure things got done. This all changed in March 1932 when a book titled *Flynn of the Inland* was published. The book, written by famous Australian author Ion Idriess, was a fictionalized account of John's life and commitment to the outback. Overnight John Flynn became a household name! Parts of the story were made up, but no one seemed to remember that after they'd read the book. John suddenly found himself being asked all sorts of questions about his heroic adventures in the inland. People even thought he'd been married before and that his wife had died tragically.

John found it odd to see his life story turned into a book and to read about his "mythical self," as he called the John Flynn of the story. Regardless of how he felt about the book, he was grateful for one thing: it spurred a new interest in the AMS and AIM, and letters and donations flowed in to support the work.

On May 7, 1932, two months after the publication of *Flynn of the Inland*, John's life took a very unexpected turn. John married his secretary, Jean Baird. The two had become fast friends, and during the six years Jean had been his secretary, John had come to value her quiet loyalty and graciousness. To everyone's shock and surprise, at fifty-one years of age, the man they thought a confirmed bachelor shed that status and became a married man. John couldn't have been happier. After the wedding, Jean moved into the Metropole Hotel with John and continued her work as his secretary.

Later that year, Allen Vickers and John went on a speaking tour together. They talked to packed crowds in Adelaide, Melbourne, Sydney, Brisbane, and many places in between. John hoped that their talks would raise awareness and funds for the AMS. That they did, but something else wonderful also happened. John and Allen received a letter inviting them to visit Canberra to address the members of the Australian Parliament. John had been praying for so long for such an opportunity as this—an opportunity to look the members of Parliament in the eye and ask them to once more support the Aerial Medical Service.

On a warm day in April 1933, John stood before Parliament. After an introduction by the attorney general, he launched into a talk about his vision for six aerial medical service bases of operation through-out the inland. He talked about how opening up inland Australia through radio and airplane ser-vices would pave the way for industry and develop-ment. He pointed out that investing just a little in the AMS would yield millions of dollars of return in the future. When he had finished, John introduced Allen, who told some of his stories about rescues he'd been involved in.

The overall effect of the presentation on mem-bers of Parliament was more than John had dared to hope for. Right then and there Parliament voted to resume financial aid to the AMS. Once again the service would get a subsidy of one shilling per mile flown. That, along with the several thousand pounds in donations that flowed in after their talks, would help keep the flying doctor in the air as the depres-sion ground on.

Through it all John pressed on with his vision of expanding the Aerial Medical Service across Australia. With the federal government in Canberra backing the service once more, John's next move was to meet with government representatives from New South Wales, Queensland, South Australia, and Western Australia—the states where the AMS would fly—seeking their approval to do so and a commitment of some financial support for the service.

As he thought of how best to go about this, John decided to target the Premiers Conference to be held in June 1933. Each state premier would attend the conference, where they would discuss issues of mutual interest to all states. John wanted one of those discussion issues to be an expansion of the AMS. Of course, John would not be allowed to address the conference about the issue. Because all speaking was done by the premiers, he needed a premier to speak for him. John decided that the man for that job was Premier William Forgan Smith of Queensland, since his state had directly benefited from the work of the AMS out of Cloncurry. With less than a month to go before the conference, John raced to get an appointment with Forgan Smith. It wasn't easy to do, since the premier was a very busy man. John prevailed, however, and he and Forgan Smith were able to sit down together. By the end of their meeting, Forgan Smith had agreed to put forward at the Premiers Conference the issue of the expansion of the Aerial Medical Service.

True to his word, Forgan Smith raised the issue with the other premiers at the conference. He talked about the positive benefits Queensland had received from the AMS in Cloncurry. After some discussion, the premiers voted to approve the expansion in principle in their states but wanted to see detailed plans of how this would be done.

As the Premiers Conference got under way, John received news that he had been awarded the Order of the British Empire (OBE) by King George V. This was a great honor, which John prayed would bring more attention to the nurses, doctors, and padres of AIM and the AMS, who he thought truly deserved recognition.

Now that the premiers had approved the expansion of the AMS, important planning decisions needed to be made. John began to prepare a report outlining how best to do this. The first thing he realized was that such an expansion was far beyond the financial and organizational capacity of the Australian Inland Mission to manage. After all, AIM had struggled desperately to keep the service in Cloncurry flying. John proposed that the name of the AMS be expanded to Australian Aerial Medical Service (AAMS) to reflect the national character of the new service. He also proposed that a federal committee made up of a representative from each state would oversee national policies, while local committees in each state would control how those policies were put into practice in their areas. These local committees would be made up of people with an interest in and commitment to the concept of flying doctors.

John was aware of one problem with his proposal. He was concerned about how to break the news to the leaders of the Presbyterian Church in Australia

that the expansion of the AMS would mean handing the service over to function separately outside
church control and with state and federal government involvement. The AMS would no longer be
part of the church outreach program. John was aware
that the Presbyterian Church had poured a lot of its
resources into keeping the service operating and that
there would be opposition to his plan. Yet deep down
he had always known such a day would come. With
the experimental service at Cloncurry a huge success,
the Aerial Medical Service needed to expand rapidly
while it still had the favor of the state and federal
governments. However, such rapid expansion was
more than any single denomination could manage. It
was time for the service to belong to all the people of
Australia. John saw this as a triumph. He was ready
to hand over his life's work to others to see it grow.

A General Assembly of the Presbyterian Church
was held in Melbourne in September 1933. Prior
to the assembly, John had sought and gained the
approval of the AIM board to make the changes he
was proposing for the AMS. The board recognized
that the scope of a national air service went far
beyond the mission's resources. Now it was time to
convince the rest of the church.

During the General Assembly, both John and Allen
explained what they saw as the future of the AMS.
Allen gave a slide presentation of his work in Cloncurry and told a number of stories. He finished his
presentation by challenging the gathered delegates to
ponder the question of whether their conscience as a

church was prepared to accept responsibility for the preventable deaths that would occur if they slowed down the expansion of the Aerial Medical Service by keeping it under their control. Or were they ready to face the reality of the church's limited resources and hand over stewardship of the organization and its growth to others?

John was impressed by Allen's presentation. Allen spoke with conviction and from the heart, and he had a deep impact on the delegates. Following his presentation, even those church members who wanted to keep the AMS under church control found his logic impossible to argue with. John was deeply grateful when the General Assembly voted to set free the ministry of the Aerial Medical Service. It was a decision he was sure was good for the church, good for Australia, and, most of all, good for those living in the inland.

Of course, John's involvement with the AMS did not end with the vote at the General Assembly. He was still the superintendent of the Australian Inland Mission, and AIM had pioneered and birthed the work of the AMS. John believed that it was now his job and the job of AIM to lead the way in the transformation of the AMS into the AAMS—from a local, church-supported organization to a national organization funded and managed by a private-government partnership. Getting to that place still required a lot of work from John.

Chapter 15

At His Finest

While John remained the superintendent of AIM, he was also head of the Australian Aerial Medical Service. It was now his job to visit the various states to negotiate and help set up separate, state-sanctioned branches of the organization. This was work in which John was at his finest. He met with Christian and government agencies, formed local committees, and wrote articles of incorporation and procedural and operating manuals for each new service. The work was painstaking. Before each new section of the AAMS could be established, a local committee needed to show it had local support and permission, or would be given permission, to operate airplanes and a radio service in that state. But John kept at it, one new section at a time. The medical service based in Cloncurry was the model for the planned first two expansions, one at Port Hedland and the other at Wyndham, both in Western Australia.

John was happy to discover that the success of AIM in the state and the AMS in Cloncurry had smoothed the path forward in unexpected ways. In Perth, Dr. John Holland became an enthusiastic supporter. He was the doctor who had rushed to Hall's Creek in 1917 in an attempt to save Jimmy Darcy's life. Dr. Holland worked hard to drum up local support in Western Australia. At one community meeting, a mayor told a large crowd how the AIM nurses at Hall's Creek had treated a serious infection in his hand and saved his life. As a result he was giving his full support to AIM and the establishment of the AAMS in Western Australia.

Despite local support and a supply of locals ready to vouch for the work of AIM, the committee that was formed to establish an AAMS section in Western Australia realized that it did not have the necessary resources to start services in both Port Hedland and Wyndham. But John had a plan. He approached a number of philanthropists inside the Presbyterian Church in Victoria about forming an AAMS section that would cover the Kimberley region of Western Australia. Victoria was a well-settled state that did not need its own section of the AAMS. The Kimberley region was twice the size of Victoria but with a population of fewer than twenty thousand people. The philanthropists, the church, and the general public of Victoria rallied around the cause to help fellow

Australians living in another state on the other side of the continent. On August 23, 1934, a section of the AAMS was established in the Kimberley region, and medical flight operations began in Wyndham in 1935.

As he went around the country pursuing the expansion of the AAMS, John sought recommendations for a pastor to become the padre of a new patrol circuit in western Queensland. The new assignment would be tough. The padre would need to build a permanent nursing home in Birdsville, oversee the Cloncurry aerial medical service, and patrol from Cooper's Basin in the south all the way up western Queensland to Cape York.

As John sought recommendations, one name in particular was mentioned several times—Fred McKay. John learned that Fred was twenty-eight years old, had grown up in the Queensland outback, could ride a horse well, and preached a good sermon. John caught up with Fred at the Southport Presbyterian Church, on the Queensland coast, where he was a home missionary. At first Fred wasn't interested in the padre position. He felt he was too young and inexperienced for such a job. As he and John strolled along the beach at Southport, John reached down, scooped up a handful of sand, and let it trickle through his fingers. "The sand of Birdsville is better than this," he said.

Following his visit to Southport, John wrote several letters to Fred encouraging him to step up to the patrol padre position. In one letter he wrote, "My own belief is that no man is sufficient for any task handed out to him, but that if he faces the task, the Great Father day by day supplies all rations as they become necessary. A man does not start out ready-made. He is the product of countless emergencies, bravely met and overcome—each of which leaves in his personality its own deposit of wisdom and power." Fred accepted the challenge and in 1935 became AIM's newest patrol padre.

In 1936 the New South Wales section of the AAMS formed, as did the South Australia section. In 1937 the two sections jointly began flying operations out of Broken Hill, with the service covering large swaths of New South Wales and South Australia.

Also in 1936, the Western Australia section became a registered company, and flying operations began at Port Hedland. During the official opening of the new flying base at Port Hedland in October 1936, Dr. Allen Vickers and his pilot were forced to take to the air in a new de Havilland Fox Moth aircraft, which they had named the *John Flynn*, on their first medical emergency flight. They flew 150 miles inland to Warragine to tend to an Aboriginal man who had fallen from a tree and broken his spine.

There were more firsts. In 1937, Dr. Jean White became the first female doctor with the AAMS. Also in 1937 the Eastern Goldfields section of the AAMS was established, with flying operations based out of Kalgoorlie. This section covered much of southern Western Australia.

One by one, five AAMS sections were established, each regularly flying doctors to emergencies to bring lifesaving help. Each new section represented hundreds of hours of meetings and presentations by John and Allen, as well as the drafting of scores of documents to meet each state's legal requirements before the service could operate. A national AAMS board was established on which John and a representative from each of the sections served. The purpose of this board was to set national policy for the organization and work with government officials. Each individual section had its own board that oversaw day-to-day operations and worked to raise money to support the section.

The only state without its own section was Queensland. A committee had been formed there to start one, and money was donated for the purpose. However, the Queensland government surprised everyone by announcing that it planned to abolish the Cloncurry service and establish its own service in its place. John appreciated the intentions of the government, but when the details of the new service were announced, he doubted that it would succeed. The Queensland government didn't seem to understand the nature of the medical service the AAMS was operating. In the meantime, the base at Cloncurry continued to operate under the direct oversight of AIM.

While John was busy establishing sections of the AAMS in various states, Alf was working tirelessly to improve the radios. He built a transceiver that had a range of five hundred miles and allowed for two-way voice transmission. The old Morse code typewriters were now a thing of the past. Residents of the inland could call each other on the radio and chat, as well as report emergencies. It was the breakthrough John had always believed would happen.

John crisscrossed Australia, encouraging patrol padres, pilots, nurses, and doctors and advising local section committees. What he enjoyed most on these trips were the opportunities that arose to have leisurely conversations with local residents, learning about their wants and needs or just spinning yarns, of which John had plenty to tell. John's wife, Jean, often accompanied him on his trips into the inland. The couple would travel by car, and Jean would take her turn boiling the billy for a cup of tea at stops along the trail and cooking their meals before they both lay down to sleep in the open, the stars of the Southern Hemisphere sparkling above them.

In early 1937, John made a particularly memorable visit to Cloncurry. Surrounded by Drs. George Simpson and Jean White and patrol padre Fred McKay, John spoke into the microphone of the mother radio station, VJ1. He told the story of how radio had come to the inland. He then switched to receiving mode to see who was listening. Replies began coming in over the radio from across a million square miles of lonely landscape. A person at Koolatah, on Queensland's Cape York peninsula, reported that before they had a radio they had to travel ninety miles to make a phone call. A person at Yunta, 850 miles away, thanked John for the dedication of the AIM nurses who worked there. Someone on Milingimbi Island, off Arnhem

Land in the Northern Territory, reported that their Christian mission had been supported by the radio for the past six years and it had never failed them in an emergency.

John was touched by the sincerity and simplicity of the thanks he and the AIM staff were receiving. Twenty-five years before, at the founding of AIM, he had set out to give the people of the inland a voice and a helping hand to address their needs. Now he was hearing their voices from across the outback and learning firsthand how AIM had helped so many of them over the years.

In February 1939, John was elected to a three-year term as moderator general of the Presbyterian Church of Australia. It was the highest position in the church, and one John was surprised to be taking up. It seemed incredible to him that after struggling to earn his divinity degree and spending his whole adult life serving the smallest of congregations in the most remote areas of the country, he was now moderator general. John also maintained his position as super-intendent of AIM and was still active in the AAMS.

John found himself busy during 1939 establishing the Queensland section of the AAMS. The government there had given up on the idea of starting its own medical flying service, calling the plan unwork-able. It gave its approval for a section of AAMS to be established in the state, and the Cloncurry base was transferred from AIM to the new section.

Although John did not know it at the time of his appointment as moderator general, the next three

years were to be some of the most difficult in Australia's history. On September 1, Germany invaded
Poland. Two days later Great Britain and France
declared war on Germany. On September 3, 1939, the
Australian prime minister, Robert Menzies, spoke to
the nation in a radio broadcast: "Fellow Australians,
it is my melancholy duty to inform you officially that
in consequence of a persistence by Germany in her
invasion of Poland, Great Britain has declared war
upon her and that, as a result, Australia is also at
war. No harder task can fall to the lot of a democratic
leader than to make such an announcement."

As the new head of the Presbyterian Church, John
had a lot to do. He immediately met with government
officials to pledge the church's and the Australian
Inland Mission's help in any way possible. Padres
took on additional patrols to free others to become
army chaplains. For the first time, John appeared in
public not in his three-piece suit and tie or his cleri-
cal collar but in an open-neck khaki shirt and khaki
pants. This was his way of showing Australians that
the church was standing with the soldiers, sailors,
and airmen going off to fight in the war.

At that time, Japan was busy fighting in China
and did not involve itself in the war that was taking
place in Europe and North Africa. Most Australians
wondered, however, how long that stance would last.
With Australia sending so many men and resources
overseas to fight, many felt it was only a matter of
time before the Japanese began eyeing the Australian
continent and its abundance of natural resources. In

preparation for such a possible invasion, Australia began stationing men and warships in the north. John became concerned for the young soldiers who were away from their families for the first time. Many of them found nothing else to do at their outposts but drink alcohol and gamble. To combat this, he decided to build recreational clubs where soldiers could meet for sports, fun, and Christian meetings. As the moderator general, he was able to usher in a new era of cooperation with other denominations to do this. In June 1940, under John's leadership, the Presbyterians, Methodists, and Congregationalists together opened the Inter-Church Welfare Club in Darwin. It was the first of many such clubs.

Much to his surprise, in 1940 John had two honorary doctor of divinity degrees conferred upon him. One was from the University of Toronto, and the other was from the Presbyterian College at McGill University, Montreal, both in Canada. John was now known as the Reverend Doctor John Flynn.

With the war continuing, John kept busy managing the affairs of the Presbyterian Church, overseeing the work of AIM, and shepherding the new AAMS sections.

In the war, things took a turn for the worse on December 7, 1941, when Japanese warplanes attacked and bombed the American fleet anchored in Pearl Harbor in Hawaii. The Japanese also launched major attacks against Thailand, Malaya, and the Philippines, all much closer to Australia than Hawaii. The following day the United States declared war on both Japan and Germany. That same day Australia declared war on Japan. The war was now much closer to home.

On February 19, 1942, 188 Japanese warplanes appeared in the sky over Darwin. They bombed Australian and American battleships anchored in the harbor along with freighters and other civilian ships. They also bombed Darwin's two airfields and many houses. After the first wave of the attack, a second wave of Japanese warplanes struck Darwin. The country was in shock. Australians had never been attacked in their homeland before.

Everyone did what they could to help as the Japanese pressed south along the coast of Australia, all the way to Sydney Harbor. On May 31, three Japanese midget submarines entered the harbor. In June, Sydney and nearby Newcastle to the north were shelled by the Japanese. For the next two months, Japanese submarines attacked coastal shipping, causing the loss of some sixty lives and twenty-nine thousand tons of cargo.

Instead of Australian troops going off to fight overseas, Australia itself had become a battleground. John offered all of AIM's resources—its nurses, patrol padres, nursing homes, and radio staff and network— to the effort to repel the Japanese. In fact, those living in the inland became a vital link in Australia's chain of protection. The patrol padres handed out charts of silhouettes of friendly and enemy aircraft by which the locals could identify the planes flying overhead in the most remote areas of Australia. Using special codes, they relayed their observations through the

AIM radio service. The whole system was so efficient that it caught the attention of American General Douglas MacArthur, who was now stationed in Darwin preparing for a major Allied attack on the Japanese in the Eastern Pacific. MacArthur often used the AIM radio service because it was, in his words, "one of the most useful pieces of equipment for communication over the spaces of continental Australia."

By now, everyone in Australia was familiar with the Australian Aerial Medical Service, though that was not the name most of them used for it. For years newspaper reporters had been referring to it as the Flying Doctor Service, and that was the popular name used for the AAMS. In 1942 the AAMS officially changed its name to the Flying Doctor Service.

John had never traveled so much. He visited Presbyterian churches all over the country, encouraging them to stay strong and have faith that the war would be won. As he traveled, he was amazed at how the conflict was transforming the inland. As hundreds of troops and supplies were sent from populated coastal areas to the north, paved roads were being built across the outback and new towns were springing up.

At the end of his three-year term as moderator general in September 1942, John "took to the bush" with Scottish patrol padre Dugald McTaggart. For several months the two of them patrolled together across the northern reaches of the outback.

Meanwhile, Alf continued improving on the radio transceivers used by AIM and the Flying Doctor

Service. In his latest transceiver version, the pedals had been replaced by a vibrator mechanism in the radio, powered from a small battery. The vibrator unit produced the electric current necessary to run the radio. Once the new transceivers were ready, patrol padres began replacing the pedal versions as they made their patrols.

Another breakthrough was made that John knew was going to make things easier for those living in the outback. The Flying Doctor Service developed a standard medical kit. This kit contained drugs and other medical supplies, all fitted in individually numbered compartments inside a large box. The standard medical kits were installed in all the radio outposts across the inland. Now a doctor could consult with a patient by radio and then direct him or her to take pills from the bottle in a particular compartment number or use a bandage or some other medical supply from a compartment and guide the patient in how to apply or use it.

With the war still raging, in 1943 John learned that Allen Vickers, who had volunteered to serve in the army, was being honorably discharged from military service because of recurring problems with his asthma. Allen held the rank of lieutenant colonel and had served as officer in charge of the Military General Hospital in Perth, which he had helped develop. Once Allen was out of the army, John quickly recruited him back into the Flying Doctor Service, charging him with setting up a new base of operations at Charleville in Southwest Queensland.

In 1944 John was saddened to receive the news that his sixty-six-year-old sister, Rosetta, had died. Throughout his ministry to the inland, Rosetta had supported him at every turn, even in those schemes people thought were harebrained at the time. John knew that much of his success was due to his sister's support and encouragement.

The year 1944 also brought good news. For his services to radio in Australia, Alf Traeger was awarded the Order of the British Empire, just as John had been eleven years before. Alf had worked tirelessly with John since 1926 to make radio communication possible in the outback, and he had succeeded mightily. The inland was no longer silent. Residents in rural areas could now talk to each other across vast distances and call for help in emergencies. Alf's transceiver sets were also proving to be an invaluable asset to the Australian military as they patrolled the far reaches of the country guarding against further Japanese attacks. As far as John was concerned, no one deserved to be honored with an OBE more than Alf Traeger.

Although John was now sixty-four years of age, his mind brimmed with new ways to make the lives of those living in the inland even better. He just had to wait for the war to end.

Chapter 16

A Man Sent from God

In August 1945 the war was over and Australia was once again at peace. The men and women who had been serving in the armed forces returned to civilian life. Now that AIM was once again fully staffed, John turned his attention to the need for a home for old-timers, men and women who had lived most or all of their lives in the inland and were getting too old to live alone. Until now the only alternative for such people was to take them to old-folks homes in the cities. Once there, however, they felt lost and alone, cut off from the life they had known. John could see that what they really needed was a community of small cottages in the environment they had lived in most of their lives, where they could be watched over as they grew their own vegetables and kept each other company. He drew up plans for an old-timers home to be established in Alice Springs. Kingsley "Skipper" Partridge offered to take on the project and guide it to completion for John.

With Skipper shepherding the old-timers project, John turned his concern to the children of the inland. Many of them had limited experiences. They could not recognize a streetlight or even an orange in a picture book. Many were shy and awkward around other children. What they needed, John decided, was a summer camp in the city. This was a startling idea for their parents to comprehend. AIM spent six thousand pounds to buy a seafront property at Warrawee near Adelaide and arranged for inland children to stay there for holidays. For many of the children, this was their first experience of church, department stores, vehicle traffic, even the ocean. The parents could see the difference in their children when they returned from a stay at Warrawee.

In 1947 Skipper took a film crew with him from Sydney on a four-month patrol padre circuit through Broken Hill, Birdsville, Alice Springs, and Tarcoola. The film crew captured the daily work of an AIM padre as he brought the gospel along with a helping hand to the most remote corners of Australia. John liked the way the documentary, titled *The Inlanders*, turned out, as did thousands of other people. Metro-Goldwyn-Mayer bought the rights to the film, and the documentary was played in virtually every movie theater in Australia and in many other locations around the world.

Everywhere he went, John was recognized as the founder of the Flying Doctor Service and AIM. This spurred him to work even harder. Although now sixty-six years old, he had many plans he still wanted to see implemented. Among them were a school of the air, where teachers could talk to students in remote areas by radio, much like the radio Sunday school that was already up and running, and a network of flying dentists to take care of the teeth of those in the inland. For the next four years, John continued his busy round of speaking engagements, board meetings, and visits to the outback.

On Sunday, April 29, 1951, while attending Ashfield Presbyterian Church in Sydney, John collapsed. His wife, Jean, and George Simpson, who was visiting at the time, rushed him to Prince Alfred Hospital, where everyone was shocked to learn that John was suffering from liver cancer. There was no point in surgery; the cancer was too far advanced. John died on May 5, 1951, at the age of seventy.

The people of Australia responded to John's death with grief and an outpouring of gratitude for all he had done in his lifetime. The national broadcasting service remembered him with two minutes of silence on the air. Robert Menzies, Australia's prime minister, said of John, "Dr. Flynn possessed two qualities seldom found in one man. He had vision and the executive ability to get things done. He was a modern apostle Paul."

John's funeral took place at St. Stephen's Church on Macquarie Street in the heart of Sydney. Following the funeral his body was cremated and his ashes taken to Alice Springs for burial. On May 25, 1951, a convoy of eighty cars drove from Alice Springs out to Mount Gillen, which John had fallen in love with on his first visit to the region. Five hundred people gathered to witness John's burial in the heart of the inland. Skipper Partridge conducted the interment. He looked out across the crowd made up of miners, dignitaries, shopkeepers, children, pilots, Aborigines, doctors, policemen, church leaders, and housewives from across the inland and said, "There was a man sent from God whose name was John. Here he dreamed his dreams under many a starlit sky. Here he worked with pride and joy in a task well done. So here he lies where he longed to be. He is not dead. His work abides. His memory is forever eloquent. For across the lonely places of the land he planted kindness, and from the hearts of those who call those places home, he gathered love."

Kingsley Partridge's words were transmitted live across the airwaves to thousands of people in the most remote areas of the outback as well as to every city in Australia. John Flynn had been sent as God's gift to the lonely places of Australia, and now his ashes rested in the middle of the place he loved and had devoted his life to.

Australia would not easily forget John Flynn. On Saturday, May 5, 1956, the John Flynn Memorial Church was opened on Todd Street in the heart of Alice Springs. Prime Minister Robert Menzies had traveled to Alice Springs to lay the foundation stone for the building two years before. The governor general of Australia, Sir William Slim, and the moderator general of the Presbyterian Church were present to officially open the building. The church was not the only memorial to John Flynn. Monuments and memorials honoring him began to spring up all over the country. In fact, there are more monuments and memorials in Australia today dedicated to John Flynn than to any other Australian.

The work John Flynn pioneered in the Australian outback continues to this day. Australian Inland Mission continues its work, though under the name Frontier Services. Padres still travel circuits through the outback, bringing spiritual support and helping hands to isolated families. While many of these padres drive modern pickups on their circuits, some use airplanes to cover the vast distances. Frontier Services also continues to offer a range of services to those living in inland Australia.

The Flying Doctor Service that John founded continues to operate today as the Royal Flying Doctor Service (RFDS). The RFDS operates from twenty-one bases around Australia and has a fleet of sixty-one aircraft equipped with the latest in navigational and medical technology. The flying doctors and nurses of the service are responsible for the care of over 270,000 patients and are the primary health providers in inland Australia.

More than a century later, John Flynn's call to go and minister to people in the Never Never continues to touch lives across Australia today.

Hill, Ernestine. *Flying Doctor Calling: The Flying Doctor Service of Australia*. Sydney: Angus & Robertson, 1948.

Idriess, Ion. *Flynn of the Inland*. Sydney: Angus & Robertson, 1932.

McPheat, W. Scott. *John Flynn: Apostle to the Inland*. London: Hodder and Stoughton, 1963.

Rudolph, Ivan. *John Flynn: Of Flying Doctors and Frontier Faith*. Melbourne: HarperCollins, 1996.

About the Authors

Janet and Geoff Benge are a husband and wife writing team with more than thirty years of writing experience. Janet is a former elementary school teacher. Geoff holds a degree in history. Originally from New Zealand, the Benges spent ten years serving with Youth With A Mission. They have two daughters, Laura and Shannon, and an adopted son, Lito. They make their home in the Orlando, Florida, area.

CHRISTIAN HEROES: THEN & NOW are available in paperback, e-book, and audiobook formats, with more coming soon!

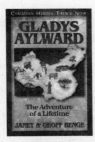  

 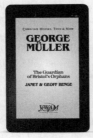 

Also from Janet and Geoff Benge...

More adventure-filled biographies for ages 10 to 100!

Heroes of History

George Washington Carver: From Slave to Scientist • 978-1-883002-78-7
Abraham Lincoln: A New Birth of Freedom • 978-1-883002-79-4
Meriwether Lewis: Off the Edge of the Map • 978-1-883002-80-0
George Washington: True Patriot • 978-1-883002-81-7
William Penn: Liberty and Justice for All • 978-1-883002-82-4
Harriet Tubman: Freedombound • 978-1-883002-90-9
John Adams: Independence Forever • 978-1-883002-51-0
Clara Barton: Courage under Fire • 978-1-883002-50-3
Daniel Boone: Frontiersman • 978-1-932096-09-5
Theodore Roosevelt: An American Original • 978-1-932096-10-1
Douglas MacArthur: What Greater Honor • 978-1-932096-15-6
Benjamin Franklin: Live Wire • 978-1-932096-14-9
Christopher Columbus: Across the Ocean Sea • 978-1-932096-23-1
Laura Ingalls Wilder: A Storybook Life • 978-1-932096-32-3
Orville Wright: The Flyer • 978-1-932096-34-7
John Smith: A Foothold in the New World • 978-1-932096-36-1
Thomas Edison: Inspiration and Hard Work • 978-1-932096-37-8
Alan Shepard: Higher and Faster • 978-1-932096-41-5
Ronald Reagan: Destiny at His Side • 978-1-932096-65-1
Davy Crockett: Ever Westward • 978-1-932096-67-5
Milton Hershey: More Than Chocolate • 978-1-932096-82-8
Billy Graham: America's Pastor • 978-1-62486-024-9
Ben Carson: A Chance at Life • 978-1-62486-034-8
Louis Zamperini: Redemption • 978-1-62486-049-2
Elizabeth Fry: Angel of Newgate • 978-1-62486-064-5
William Wilberforce: Take Up the Fight • 978-1-62486-057-7
William Bradford: Plymouth's Rock • 978-1-62486-092-8

Christian Heroes: Then & Now

Gladys Aylward: The Adventure of a Lifetime • 978-1-57658-019-6
Nate Saint: On a Wing and a Prayer • 978-1-57658-017-2
Hudson Taylor: Deep in the Heart of China • 978-1-57658-016-5
Amy Carmichael: Rescuer of Precious Gems • 978-1-57658-018-9
Eric Liddell: Something Greater Than Gold • 978-1-57658-137-7
Corrie ten Boom: Keeper of the Angels' Den • 978-1-57658-136-0

William Carey: Obliged to Go • 978-1-57658-147-6
George Müller: Guardian of Bristol's Orphans • 978-1-57658-145-2
Jim Elliot: One Great Purpose • 978-1-57658-146-9
Mary Slessor: Forward into Calabar • 978-1-57658-148-3
David Livingstone: Africa's Trailblazer • 978-1-57658-153-7
Betty Greene: Wings to Serve • 978-1-57658-152-0
Adoniram Judson: Bound for Burma • 978-1-57658-161-2
Cameron Townsend: Good News in Every Language • 978-1-57658-164-3
Jonathan Goforth: An Open Door in China • 978-1-57658-174-2
Lottie Moon: Giving Her All for China • 978-1-57658-188-9
John Williams: Messenger of Peace • 978-1-57658-256-5
William Booth: Soup, Soap, and Salvation • 978-1-57658-258-9
Rowland Bingham: Into Africa's Interior • 978-1-57658-282-4
Ida Scudder: Healing Bodies, Touching Hearts • 978-1-57658-285-5
Wilfred Grenfell: Fisher of Men • 978-1-57658-292-3
Lillian Trasher: The Greatest Wonder in Egypt • 978-1-57658-305-0
Loren Cunningham: Into All the World • 978-1-57658-199-5
Florence Young: Mission Accomplished • 978-1-57658-313-5
Sundar Singh: Footprints Over the Mountains • 978-1-57658-318-0
C. T. Studd: No Retreat • 978-1-57658-288-6
Rachel Saint: A Star in the Jungle • 978-1-57658-337-1
Brother Andrew: God's Secret Agent • 978-1-57658-355-5
Clarence Jones: Mr. Radio • 978-1-57658-343-2
Count Zinzendorf: Firstfruit • 978-1-57658-262-6
John Wesley: The World His Parish • 978-1-57658-382-1
C. S. Lewis: Master Storyteller • 978-1-57658-385-2
David Bussau: Facing the World Head-on • 978-1-57658-415-6
Jacob DeShazer: Forgive Your Enemies • 978-1-57658-475-0
Isobel Kuhn: On the Roof of the World • 978-1-57658-497-2
Elisabeth Elliot: Joyful Surrender • 978-1-57658-513-9
Paul Brand: Helping Hands • 978-1-57658-536-8
D. L. Moody: Bringing Souls to Christ • 978-1-57658-552-8
Dietrich Bonhoeffer: In the Midst of Wickedness • 978-1-57658-713-3
Francis Asbury: Circuit Rider • 978-1-57658-737-9
Samuel Zwemer: The Burden of Arabia • 978-1-57658-738-6
Klaus-Dieter John: Hope in the Land of the Incas • 978-1-57658-826-2
Mildred Cable: Through the Jade Gate • 978-157658-886-4
John Flynn: Into the Never Never • 978-1-57658-898-7

Available in paperback, e-book, and audiobook formats.
Unit Study Curriculum Guides are available for many biographies.
www.HeroesThenAndNow.com